Peaceful Mandalas

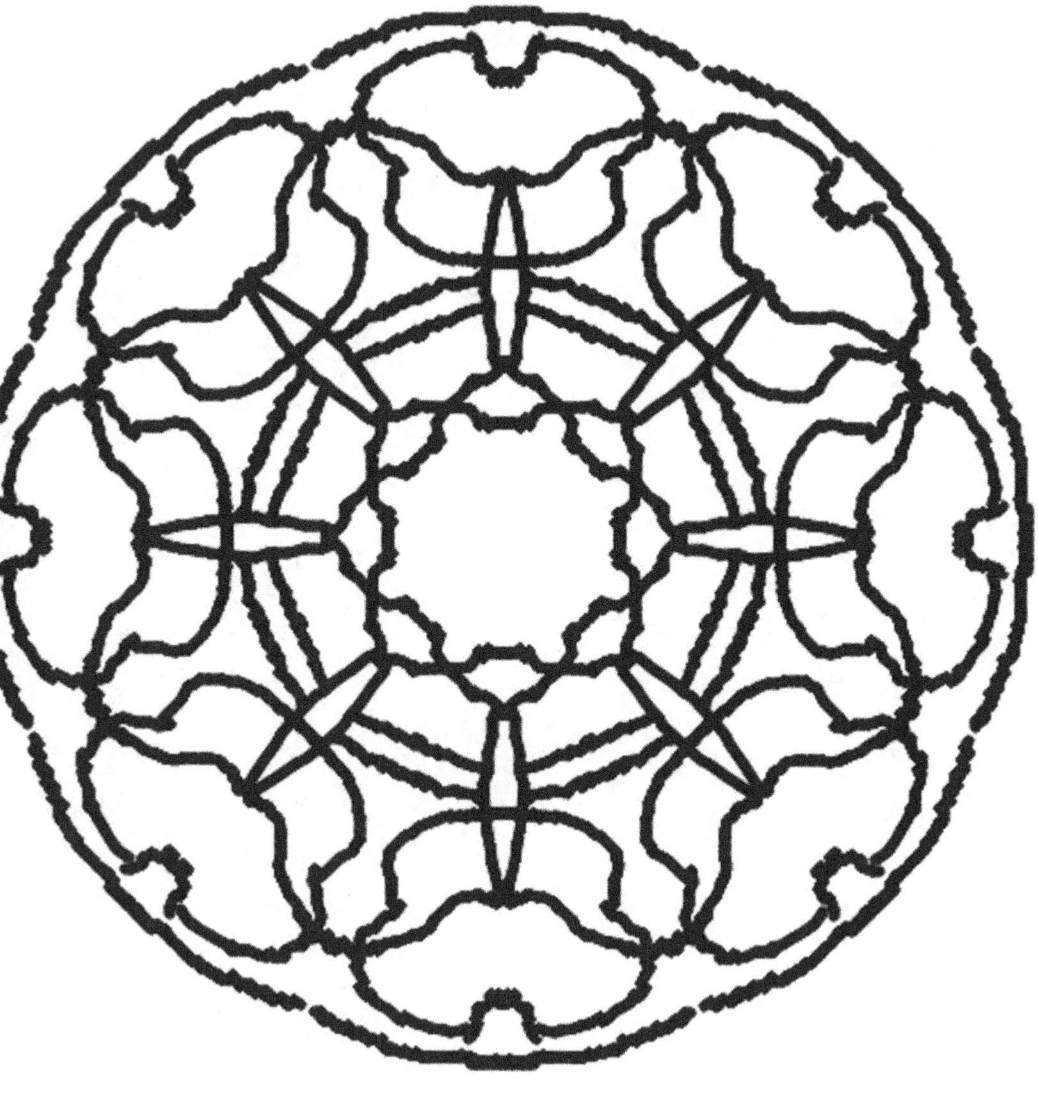

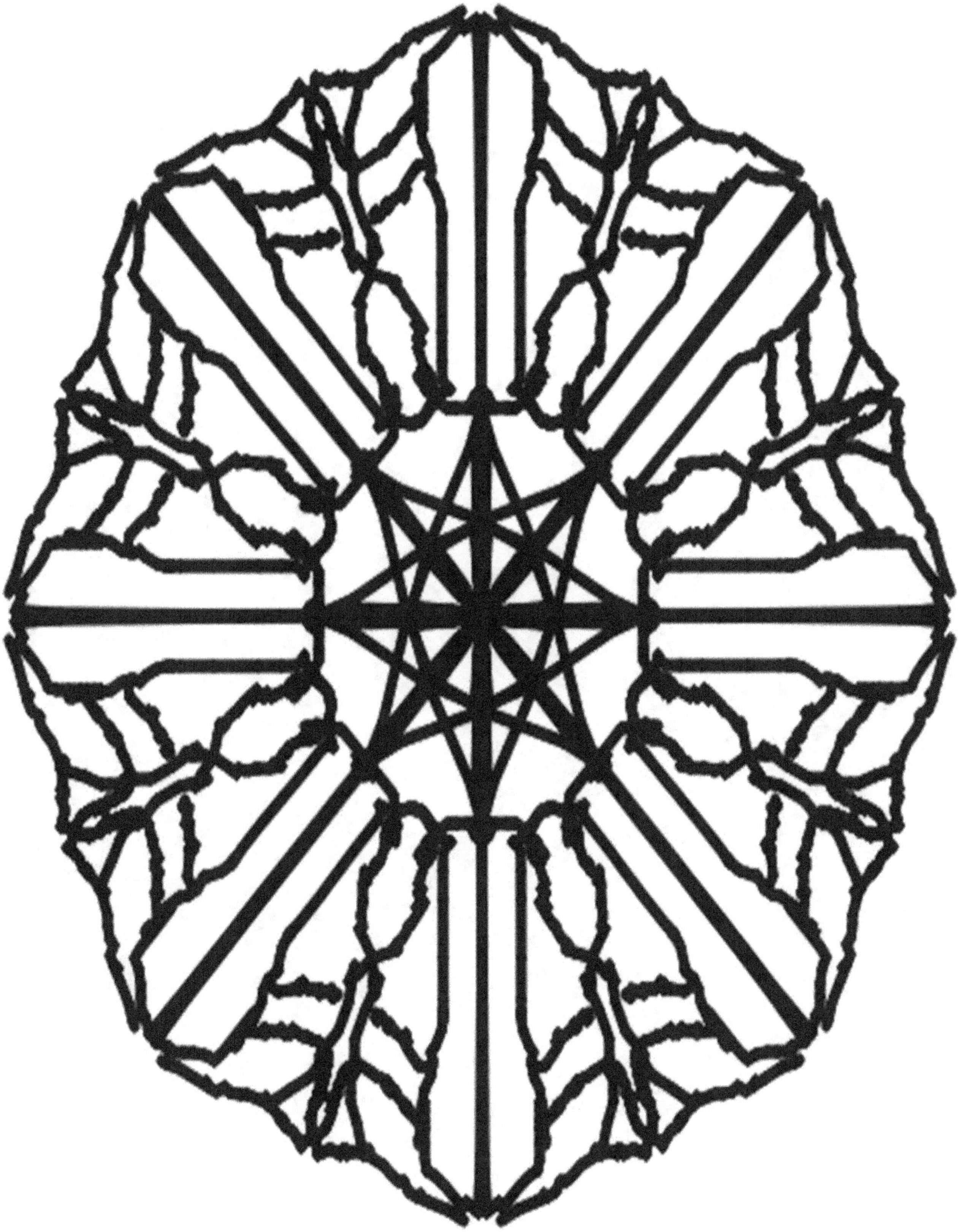

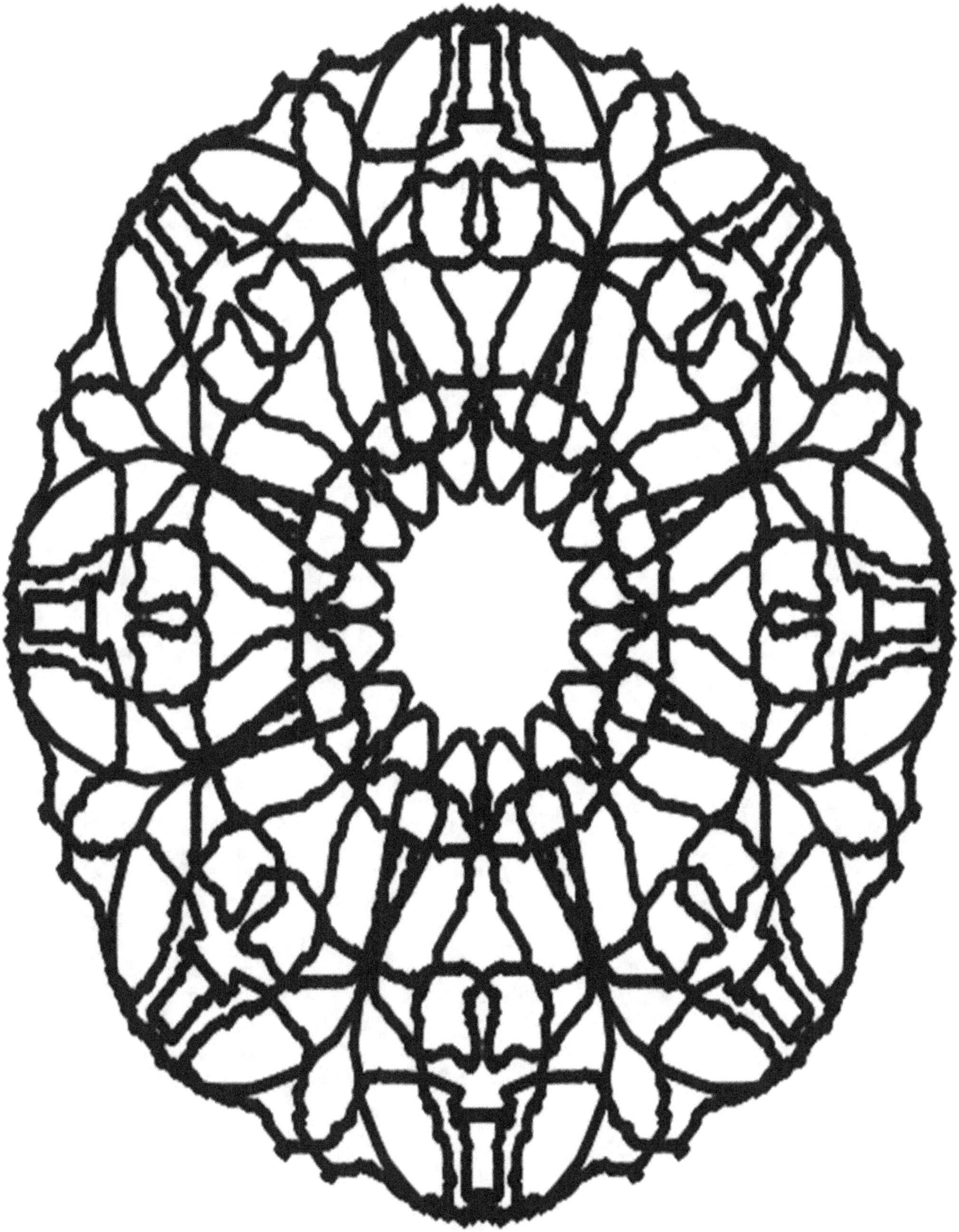

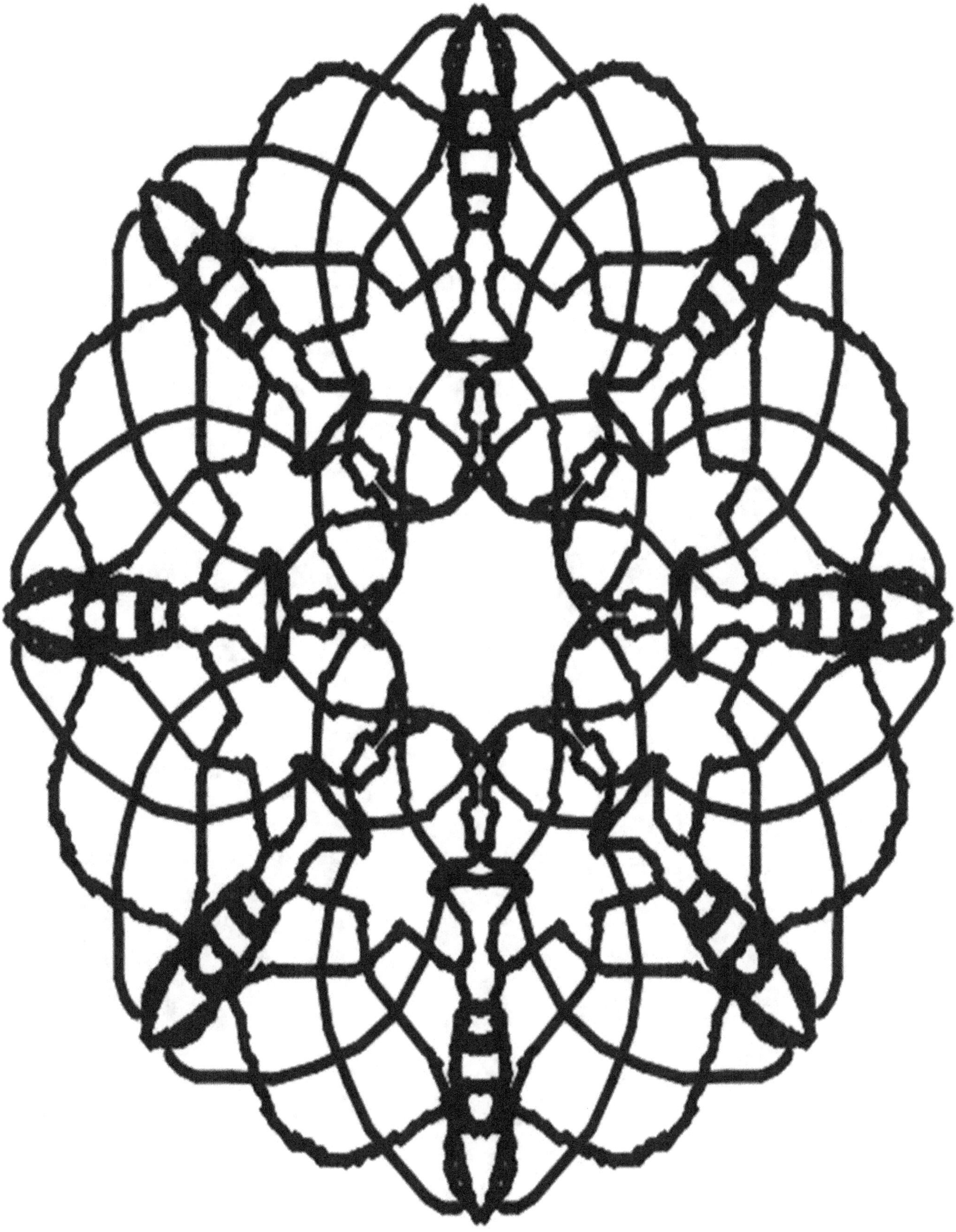

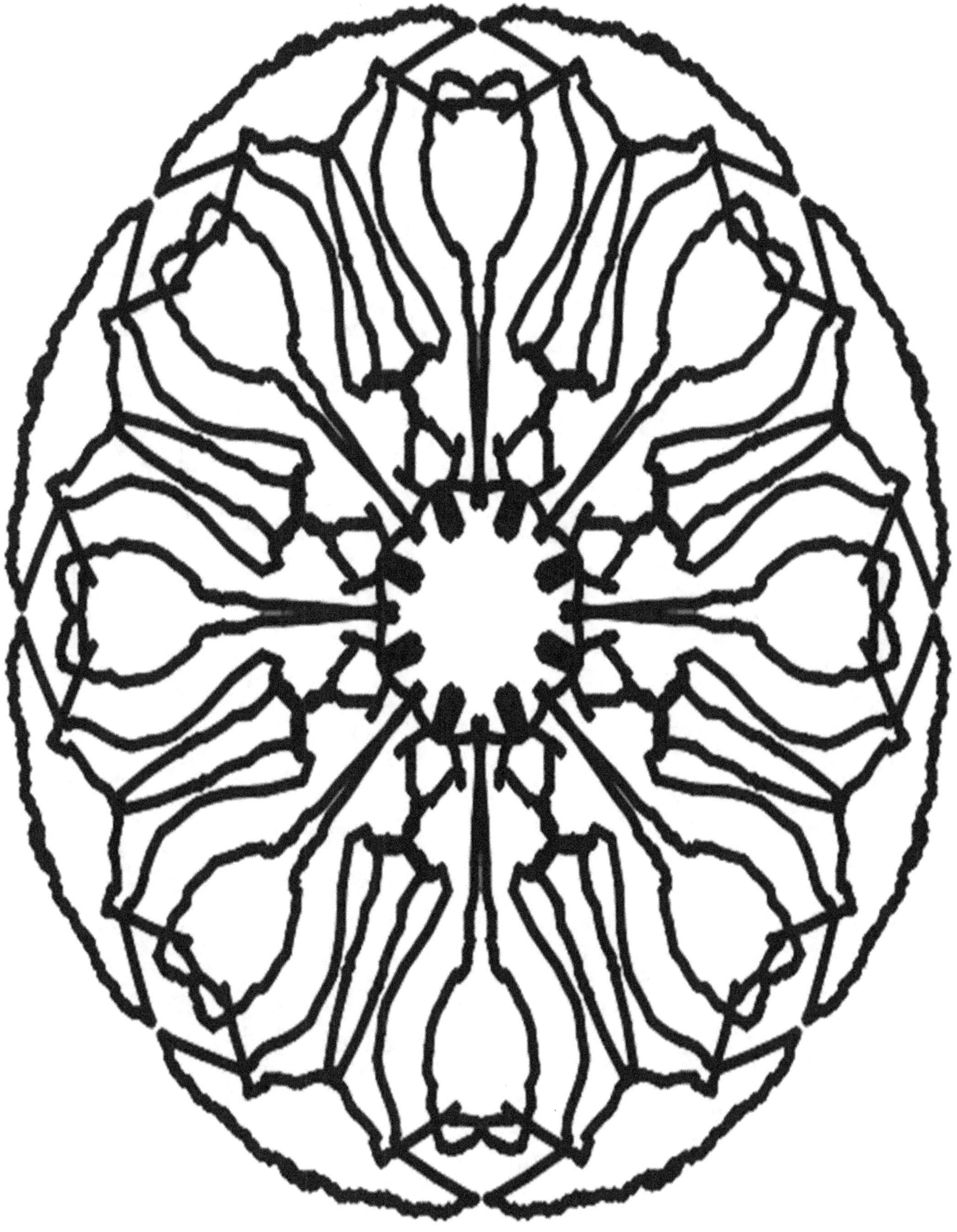

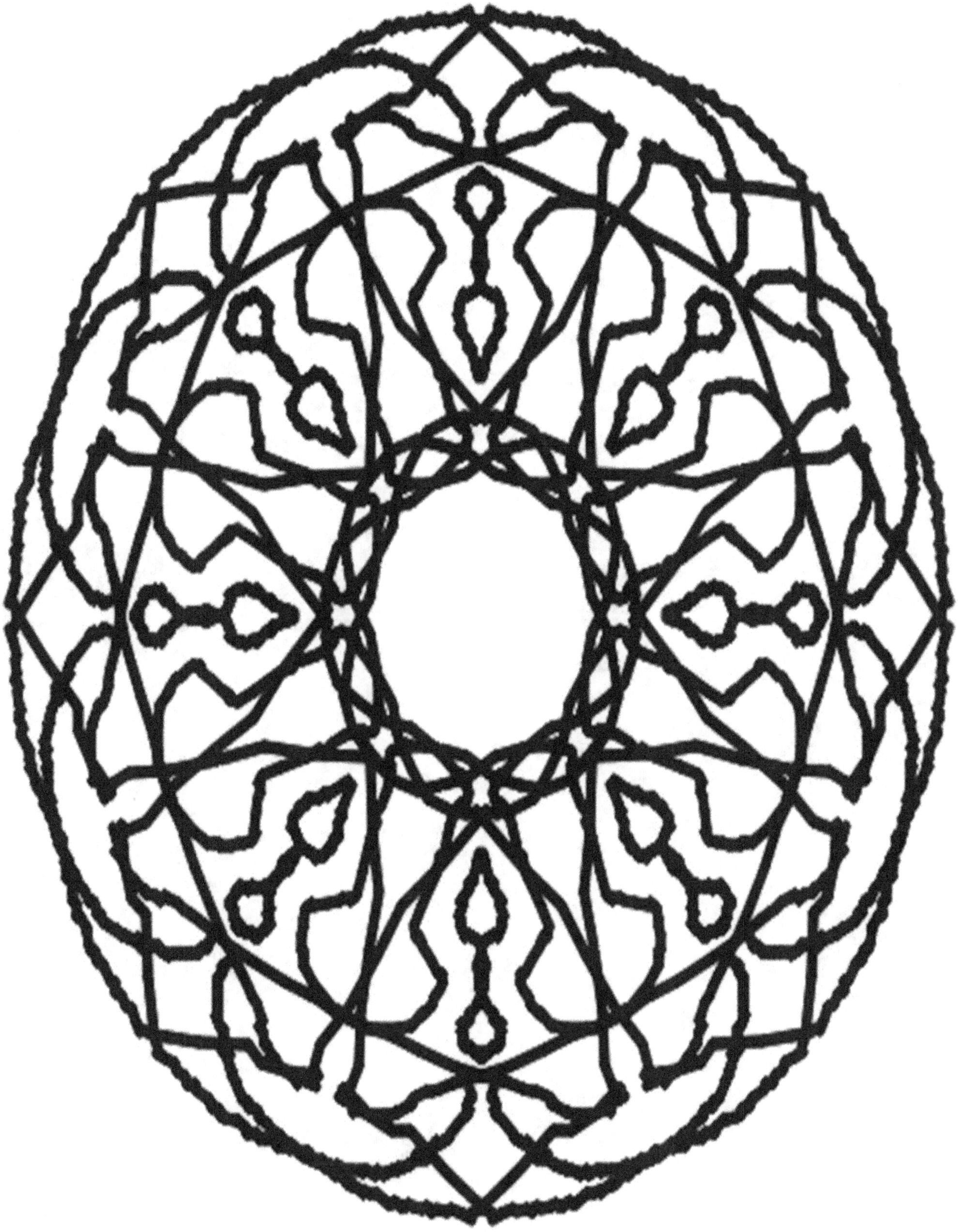

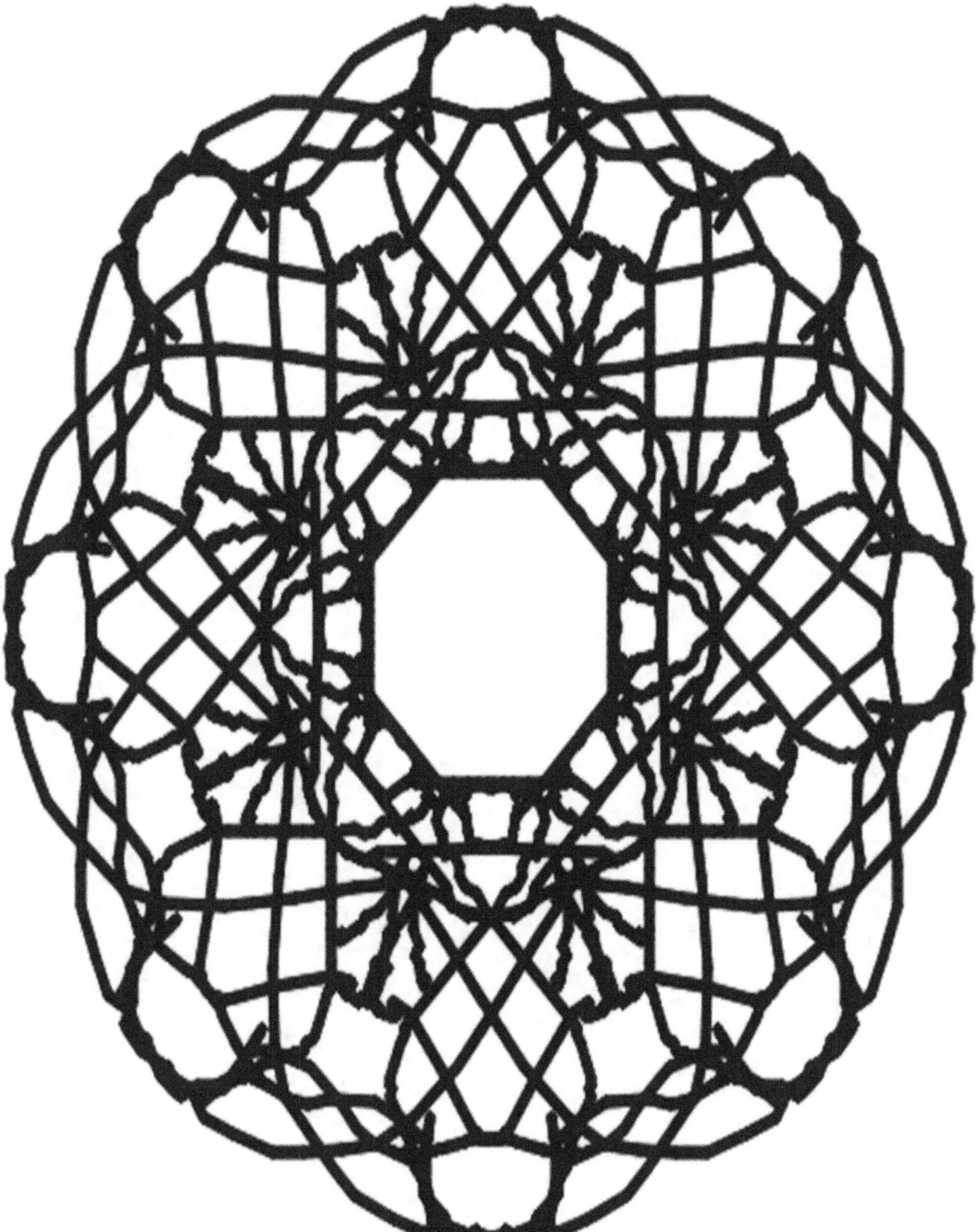

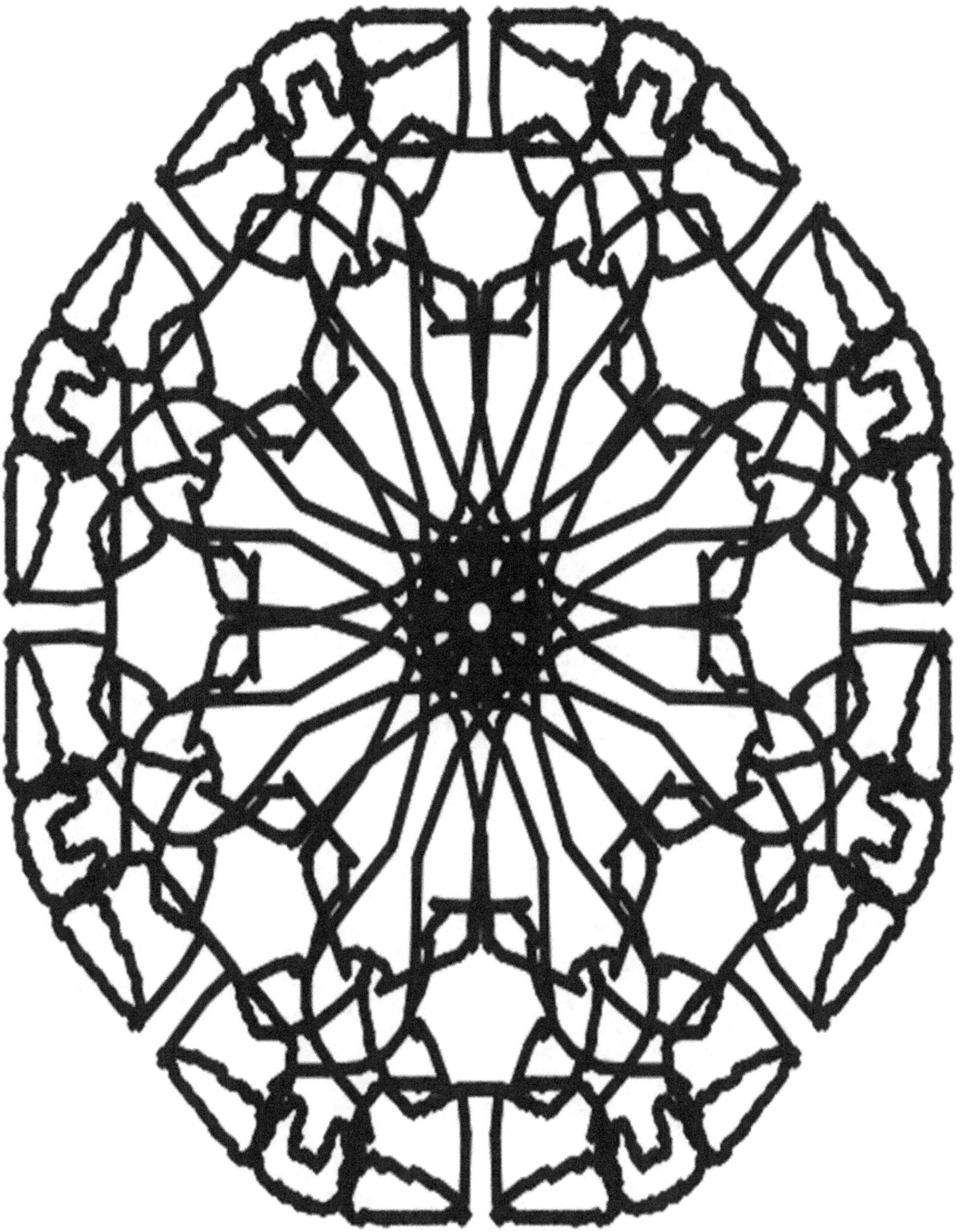

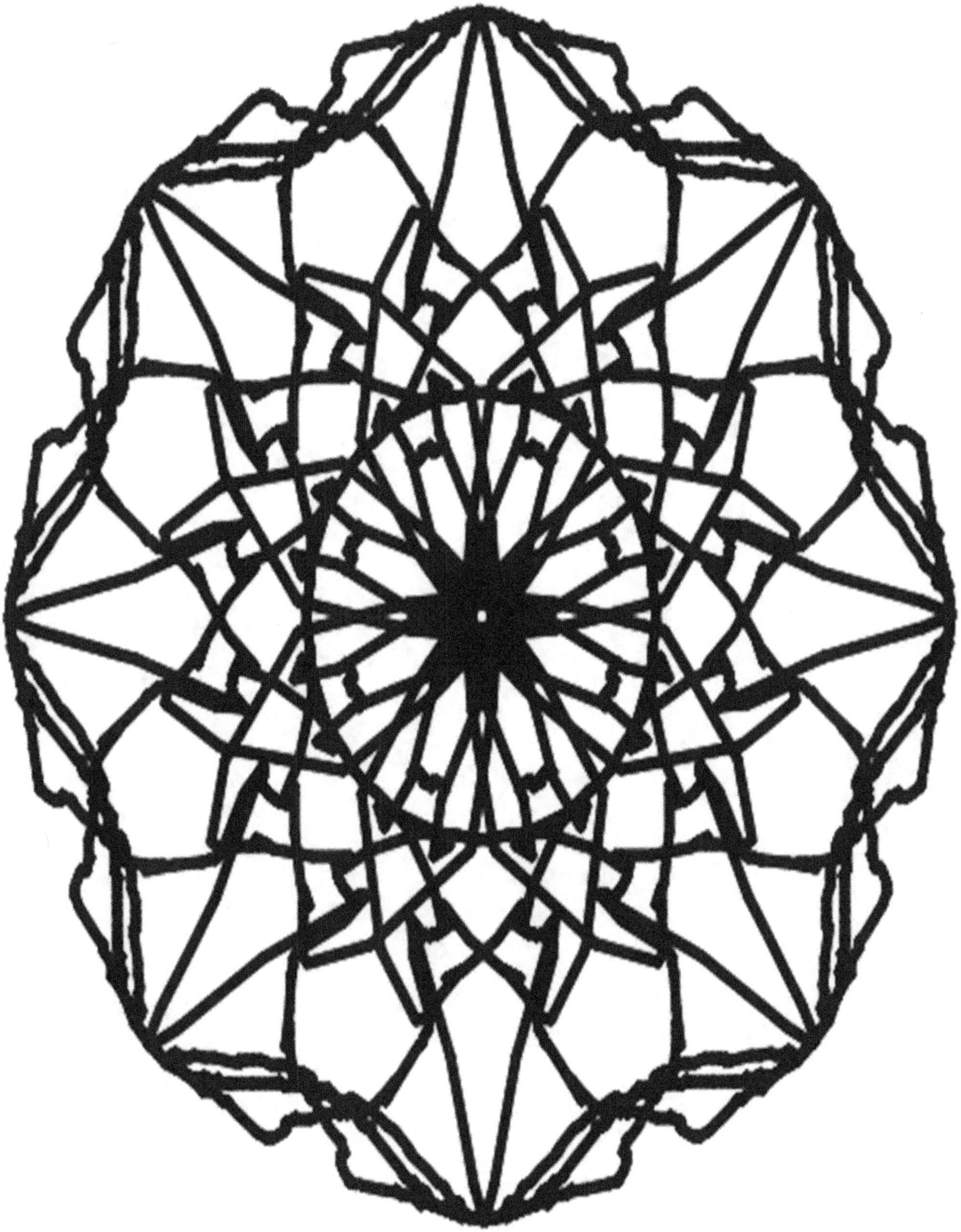

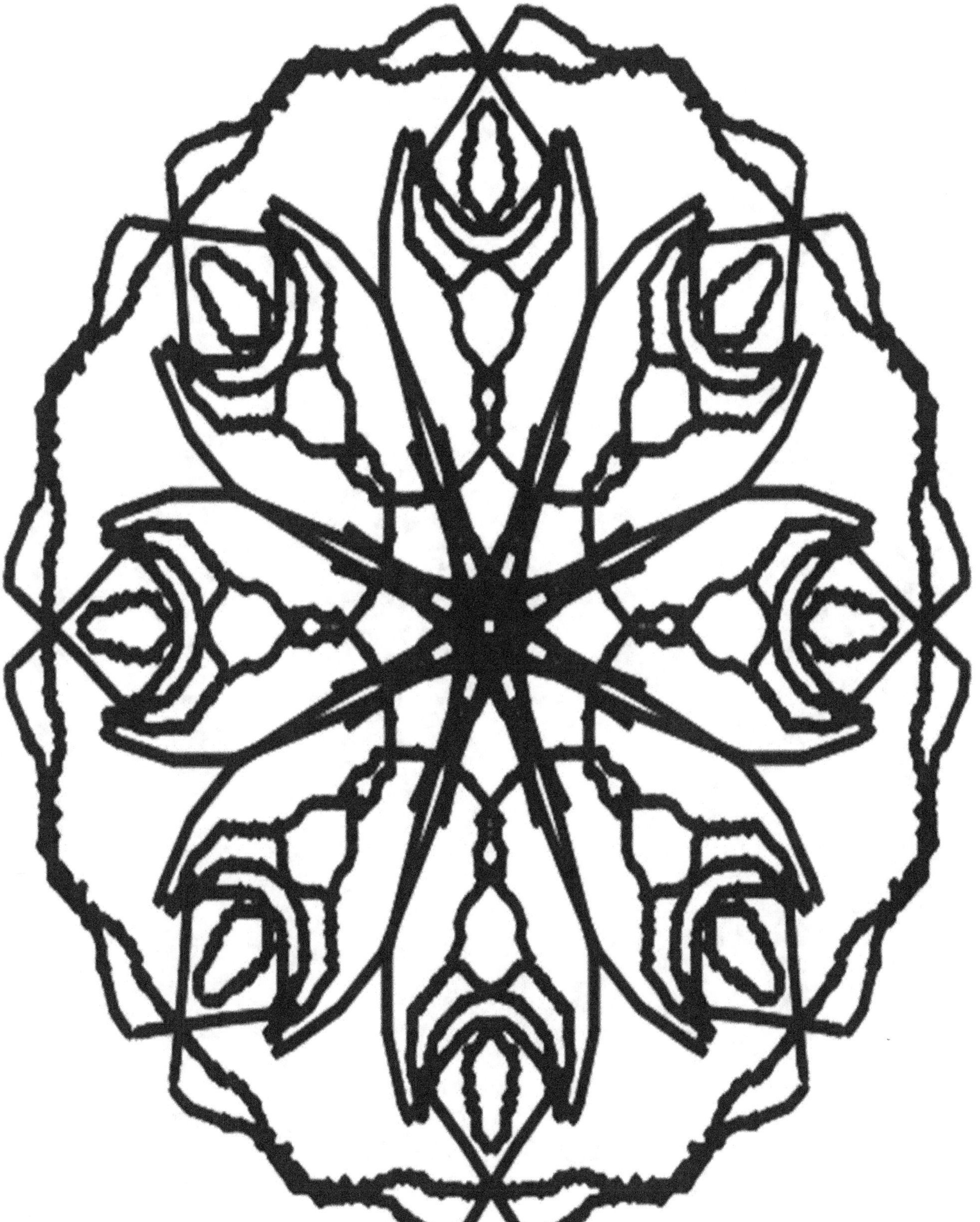

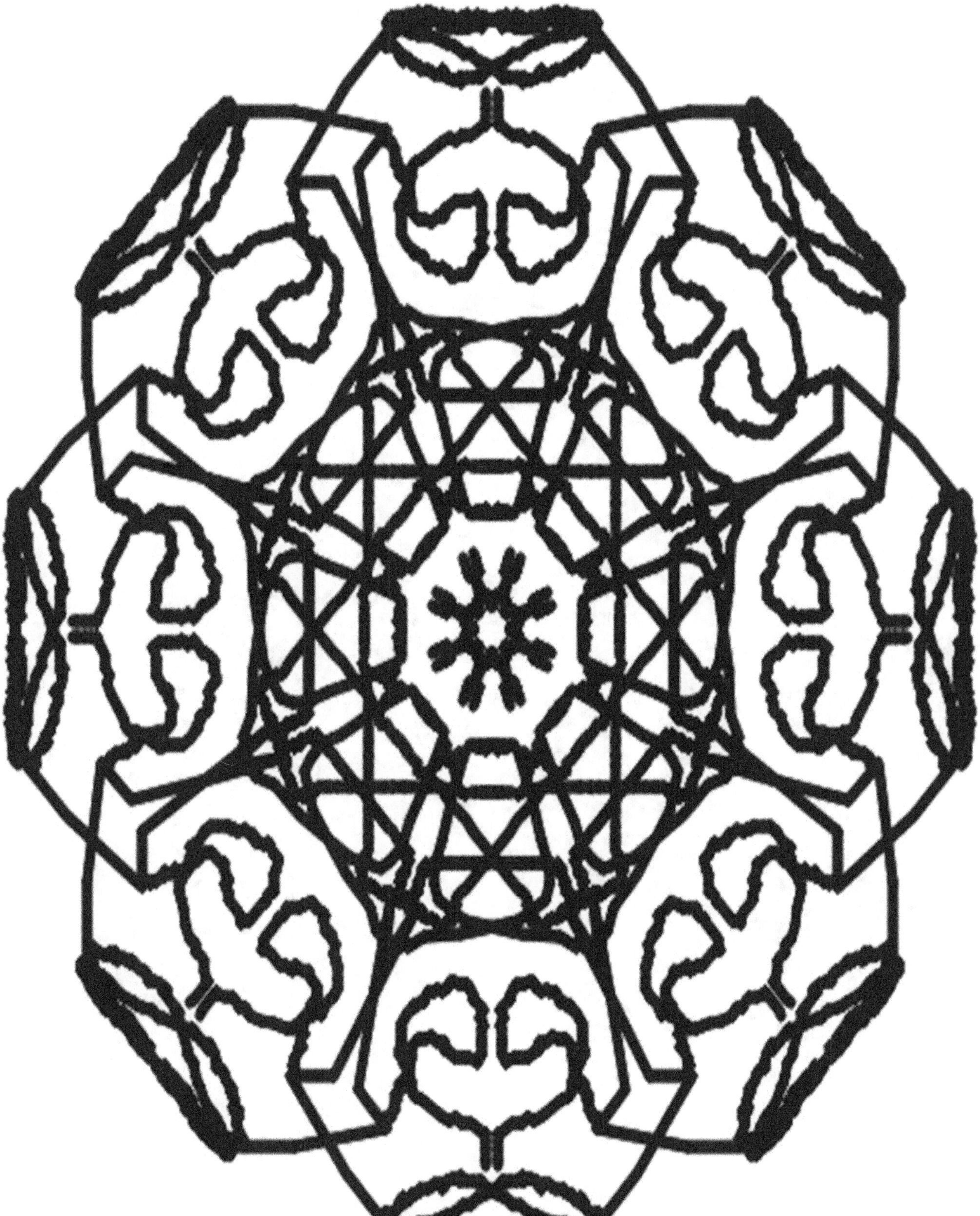

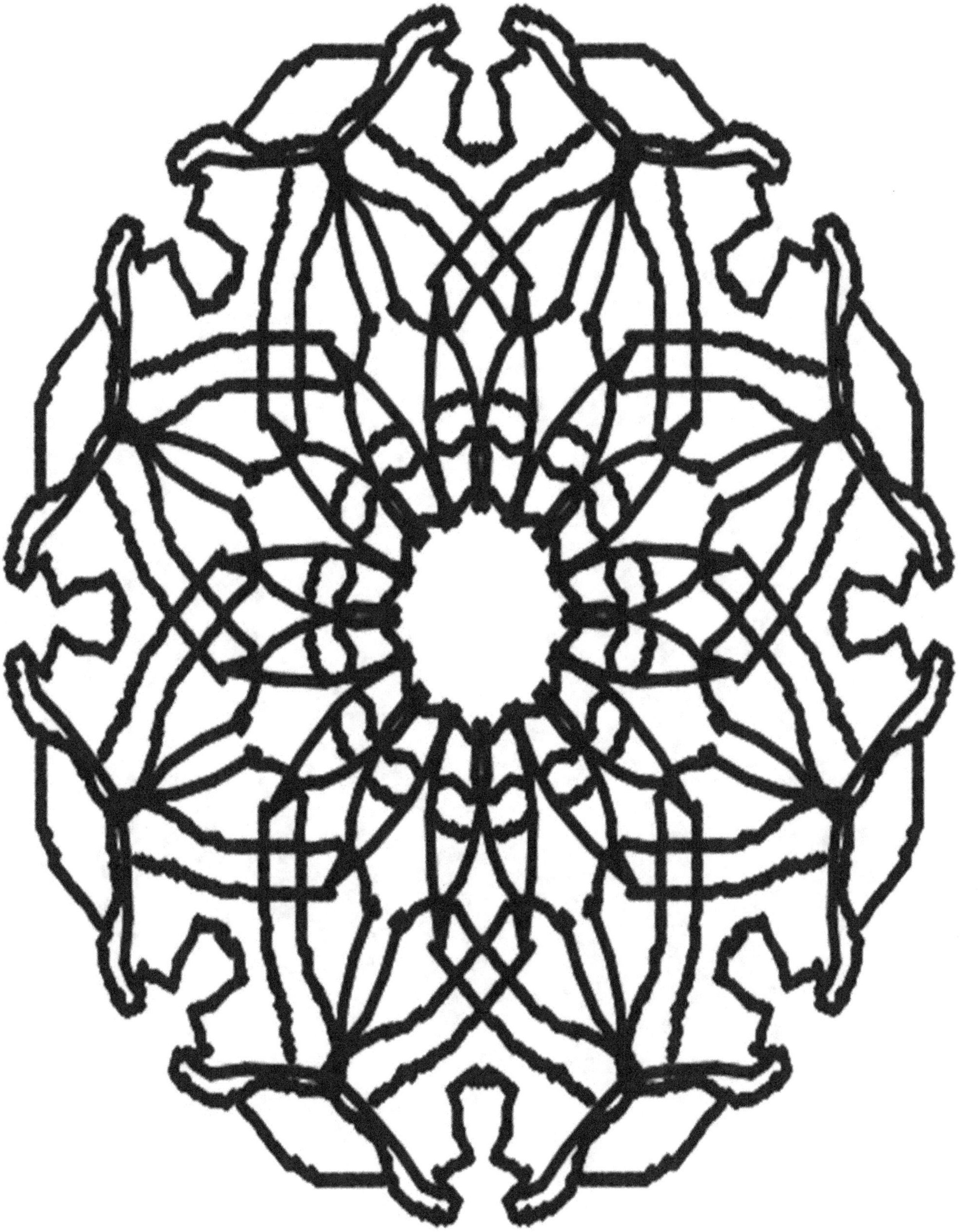

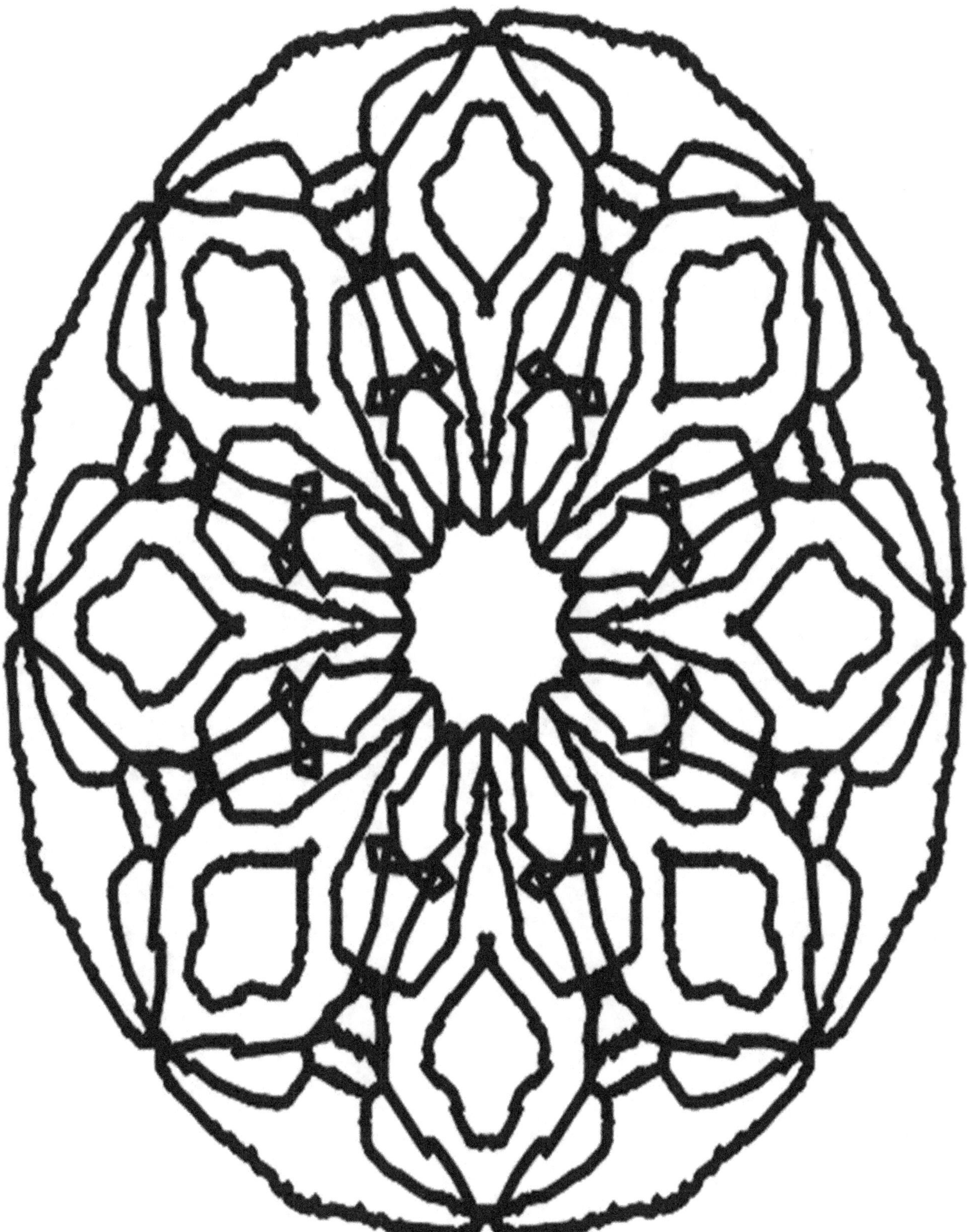

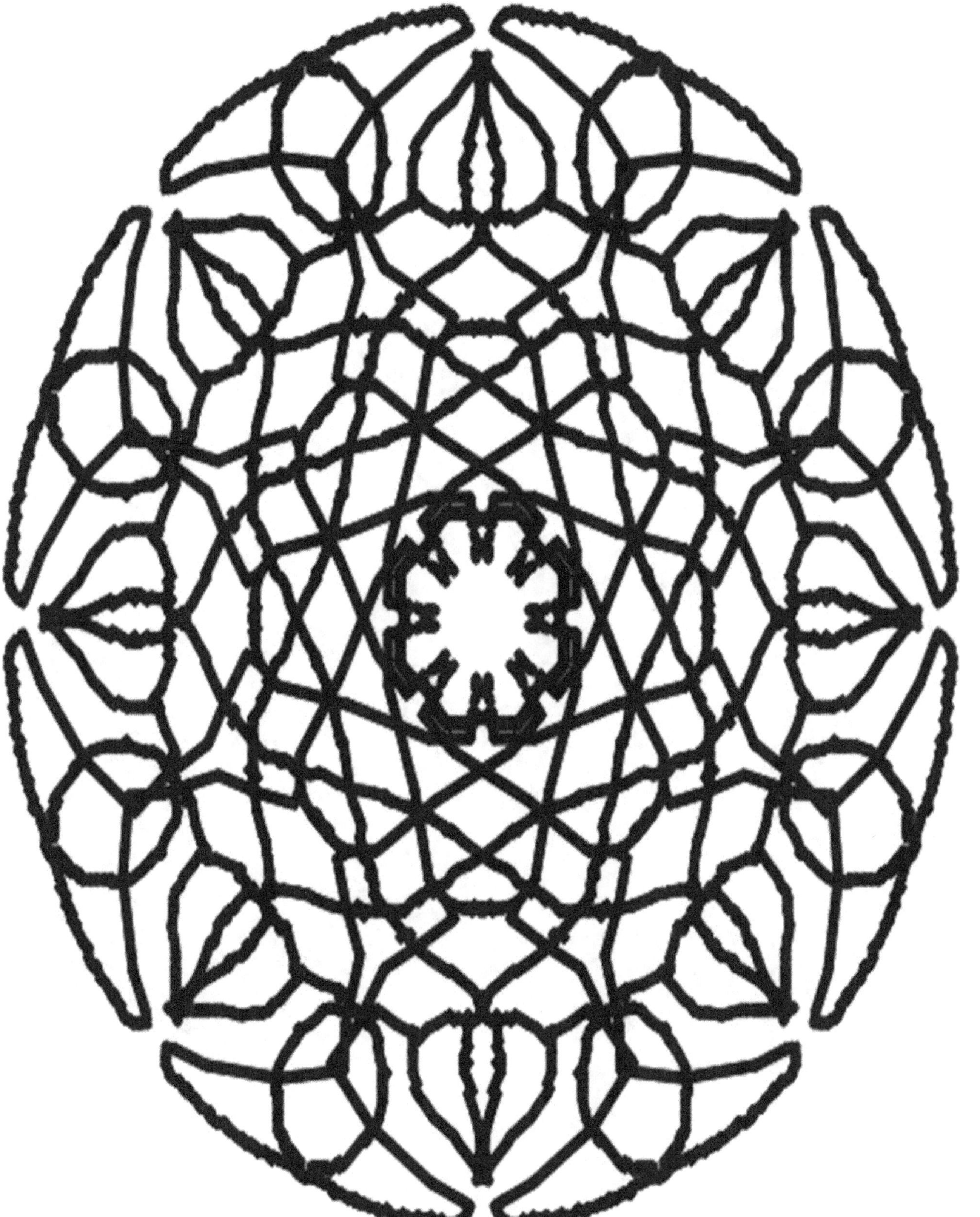

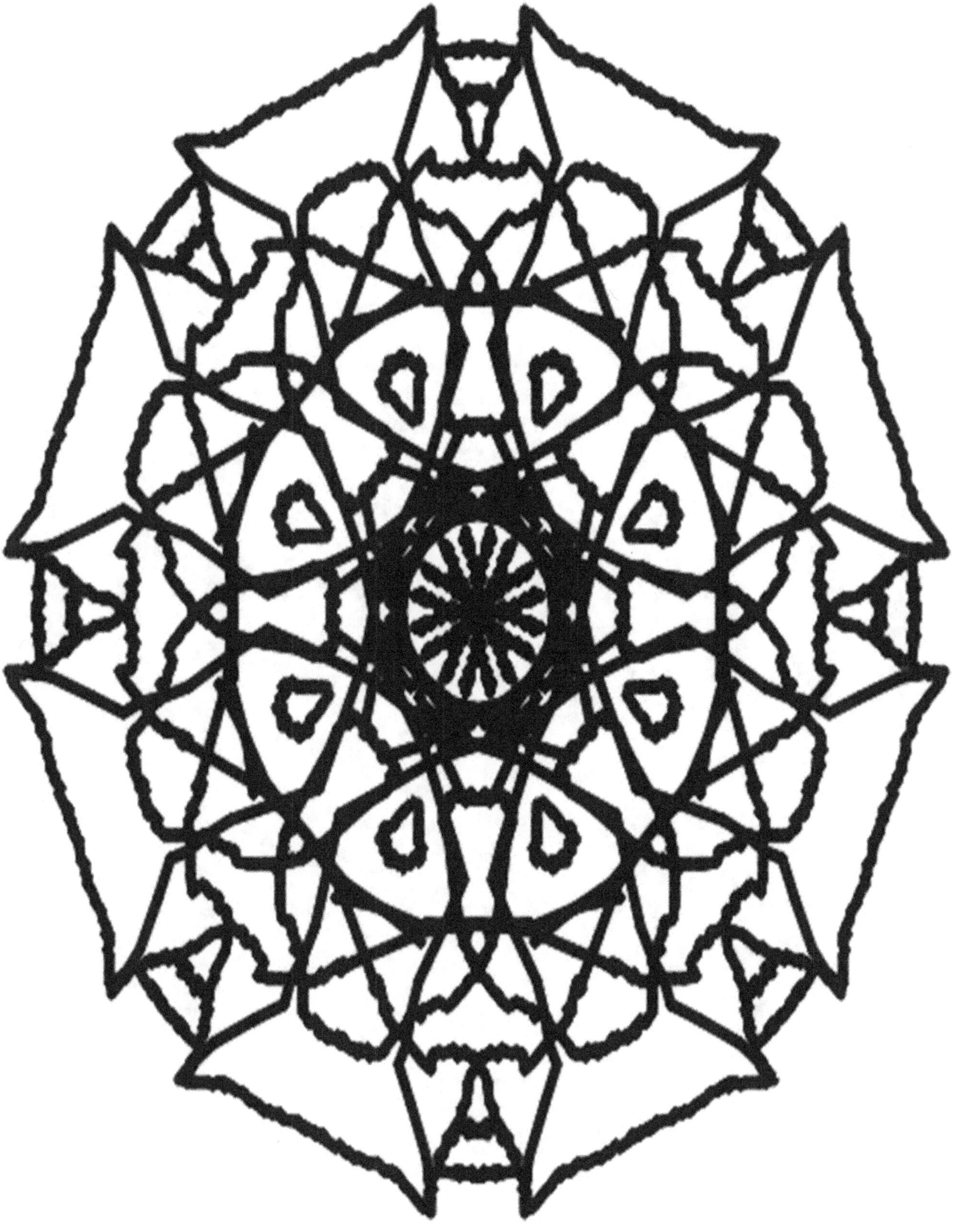

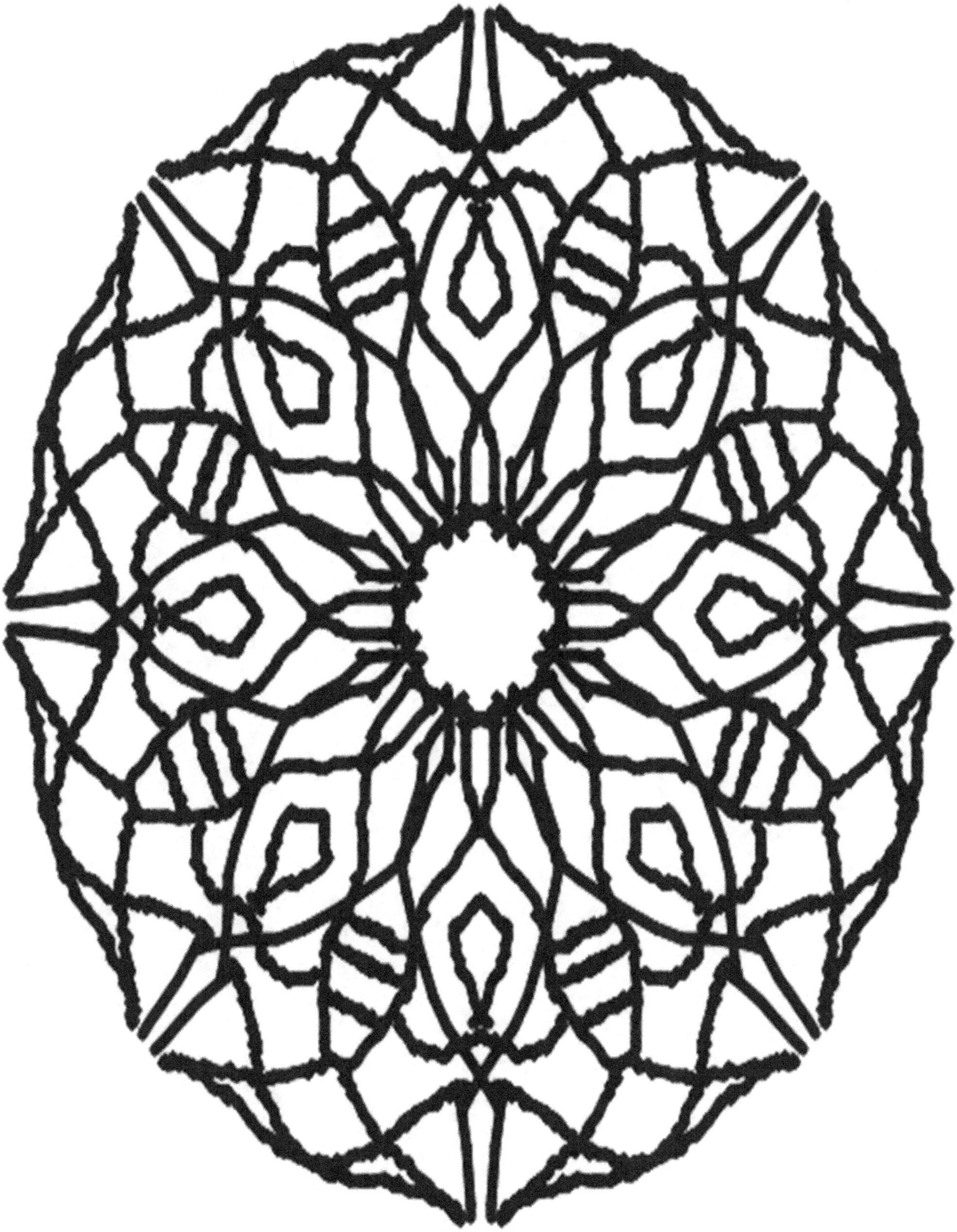

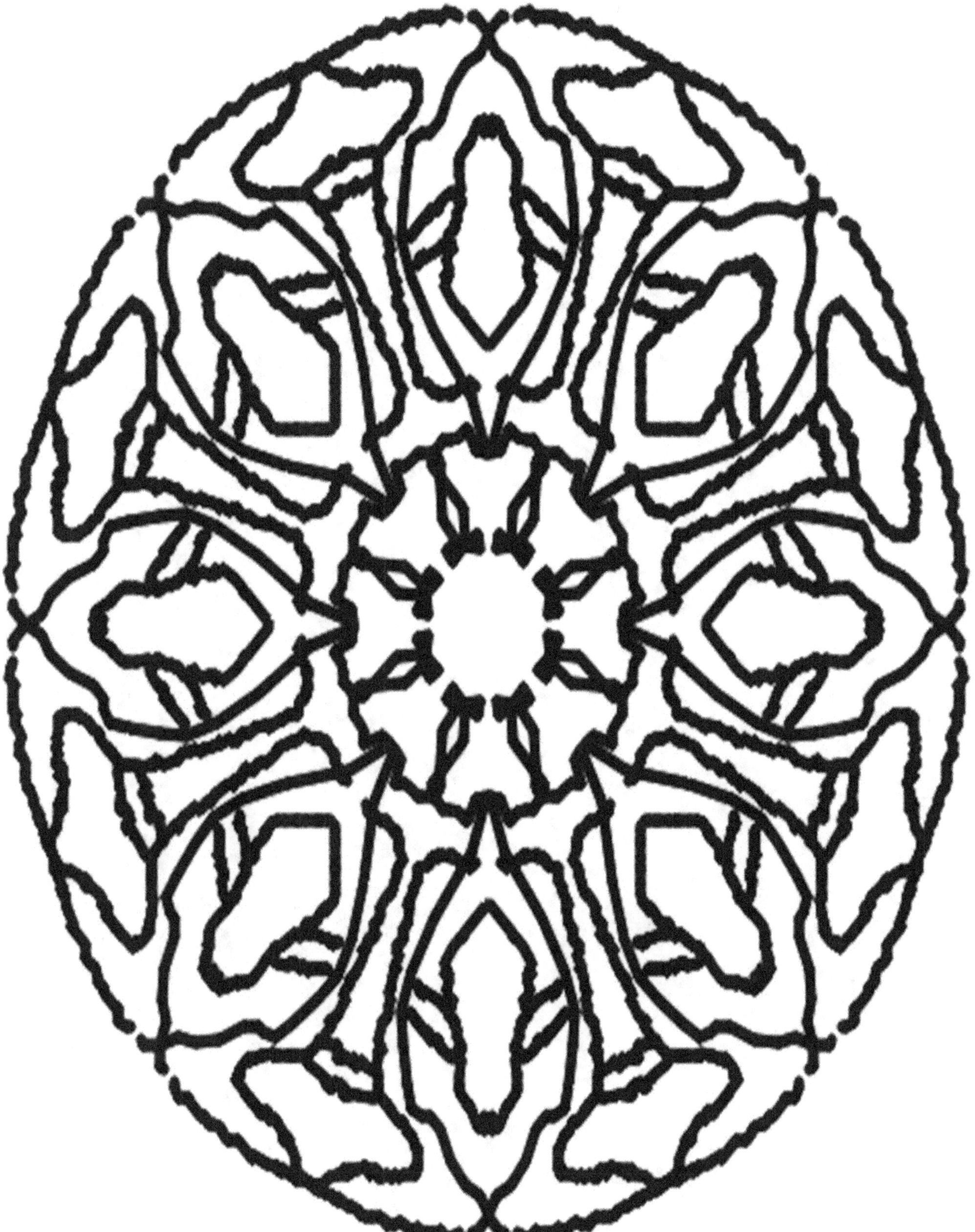

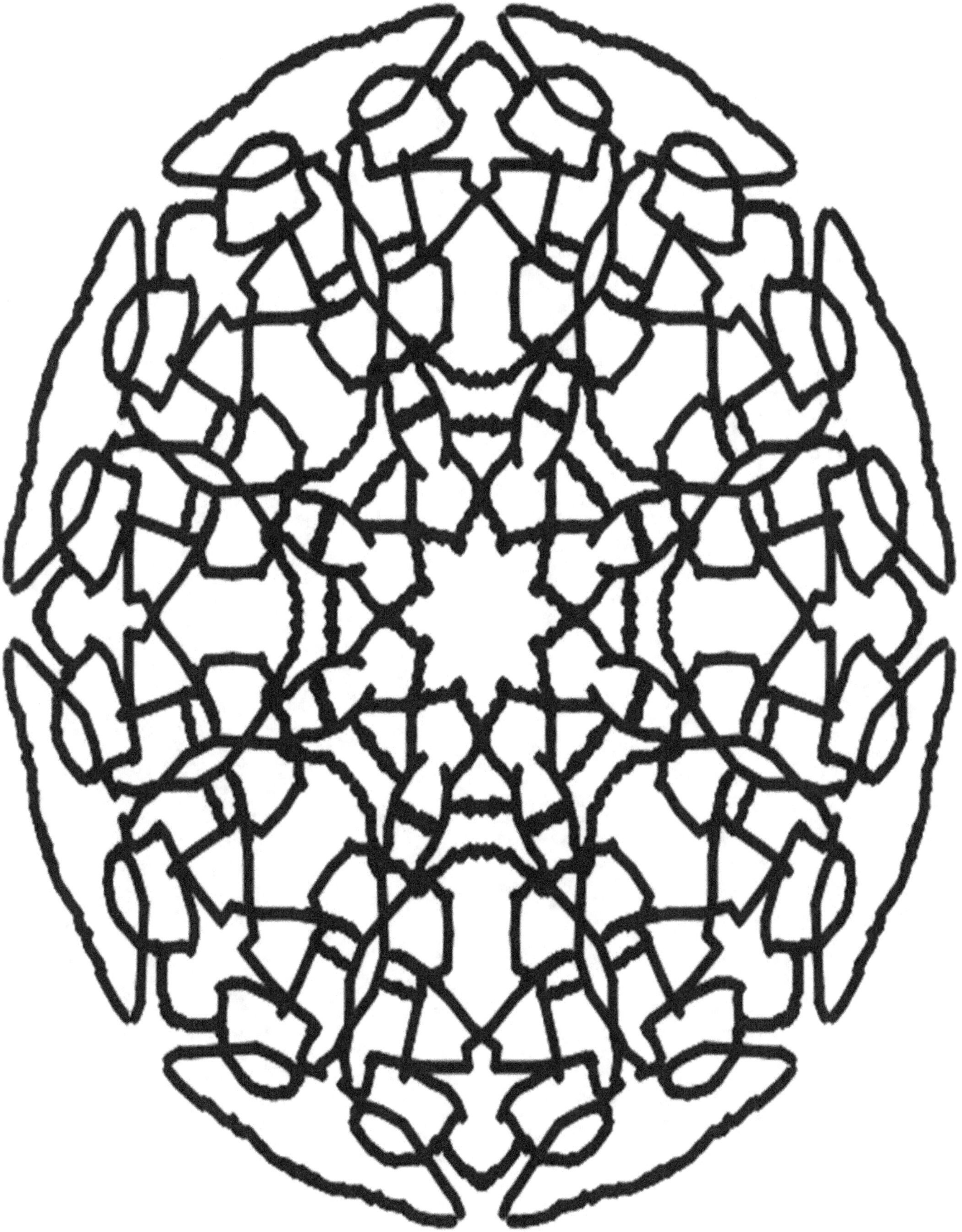

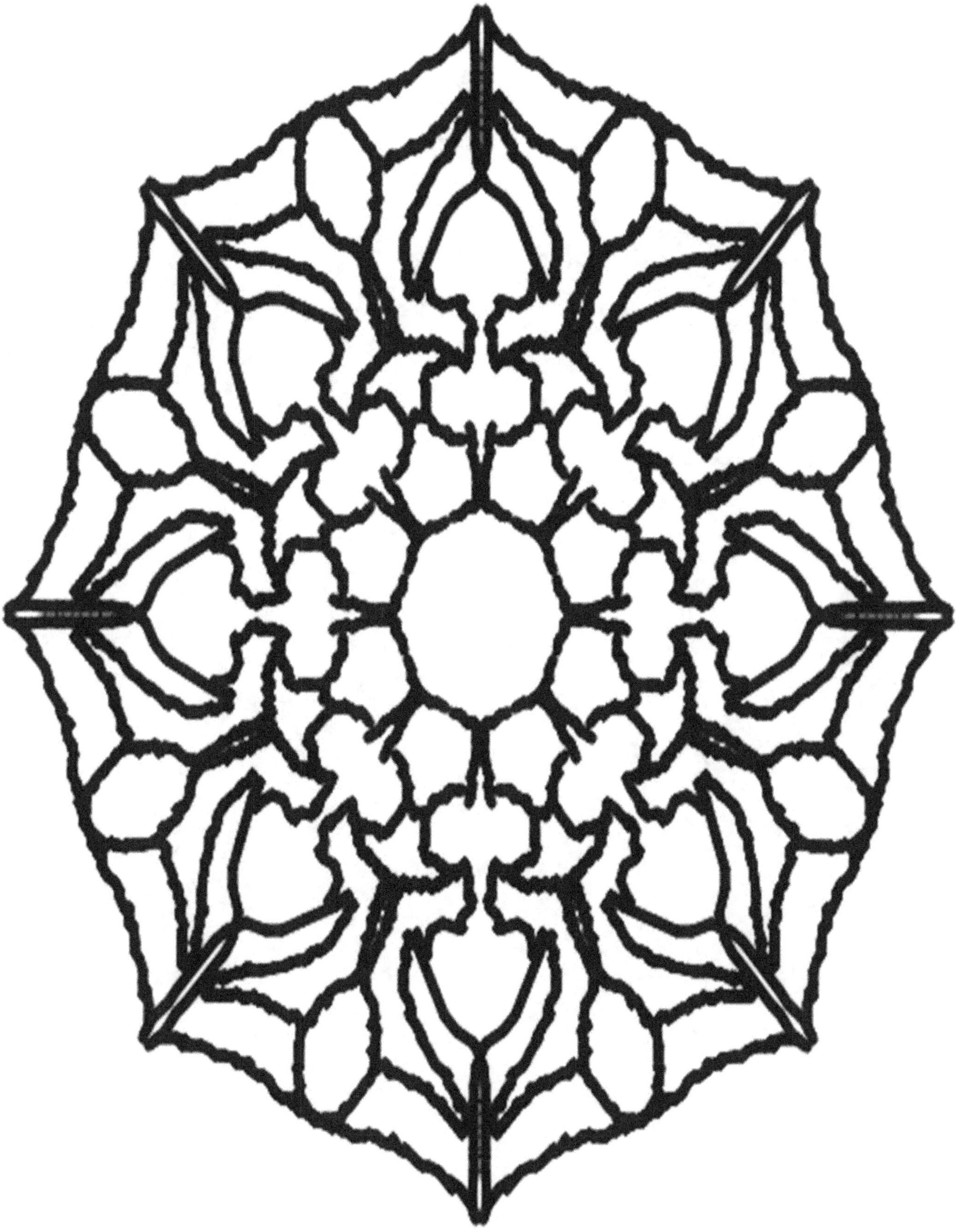

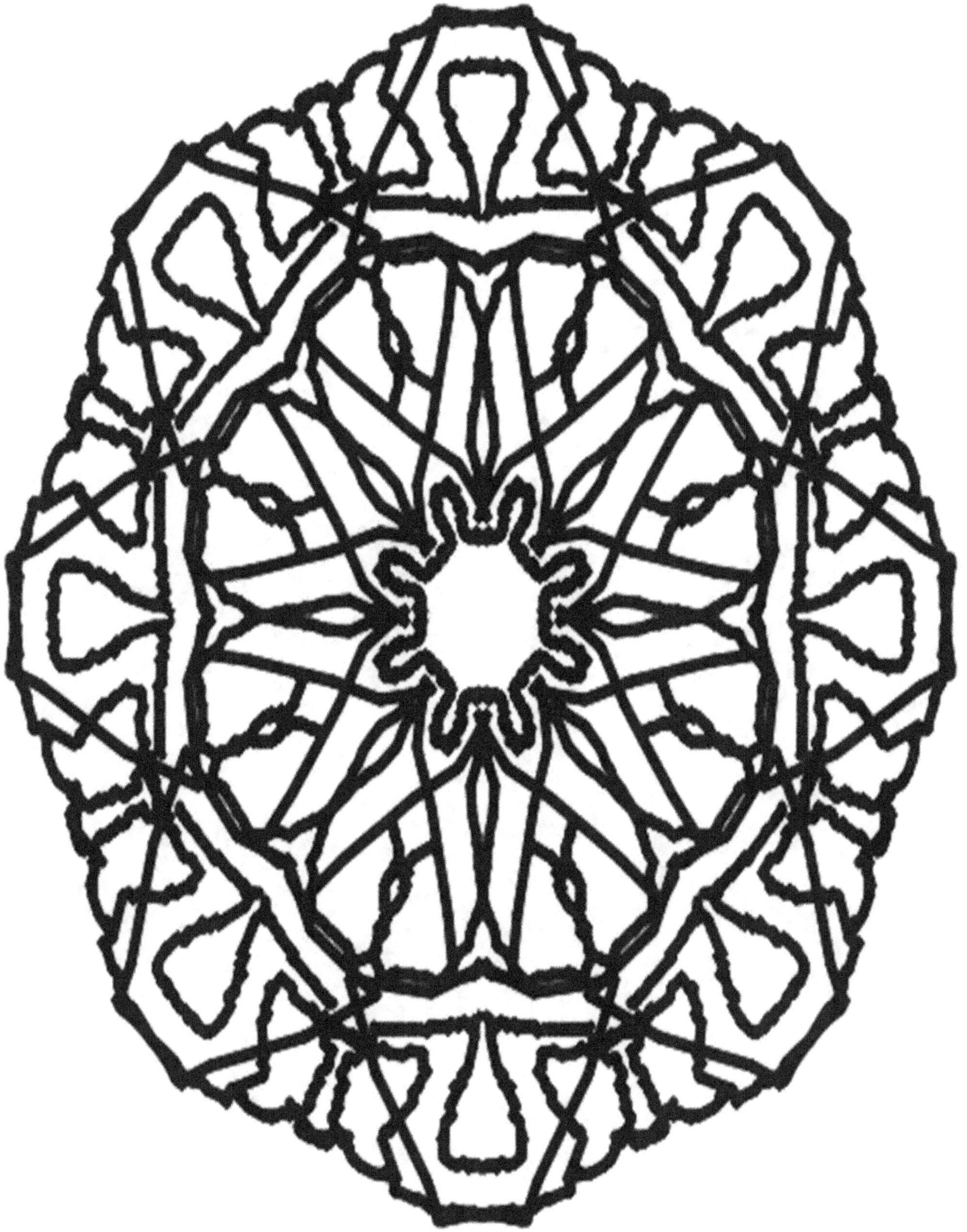

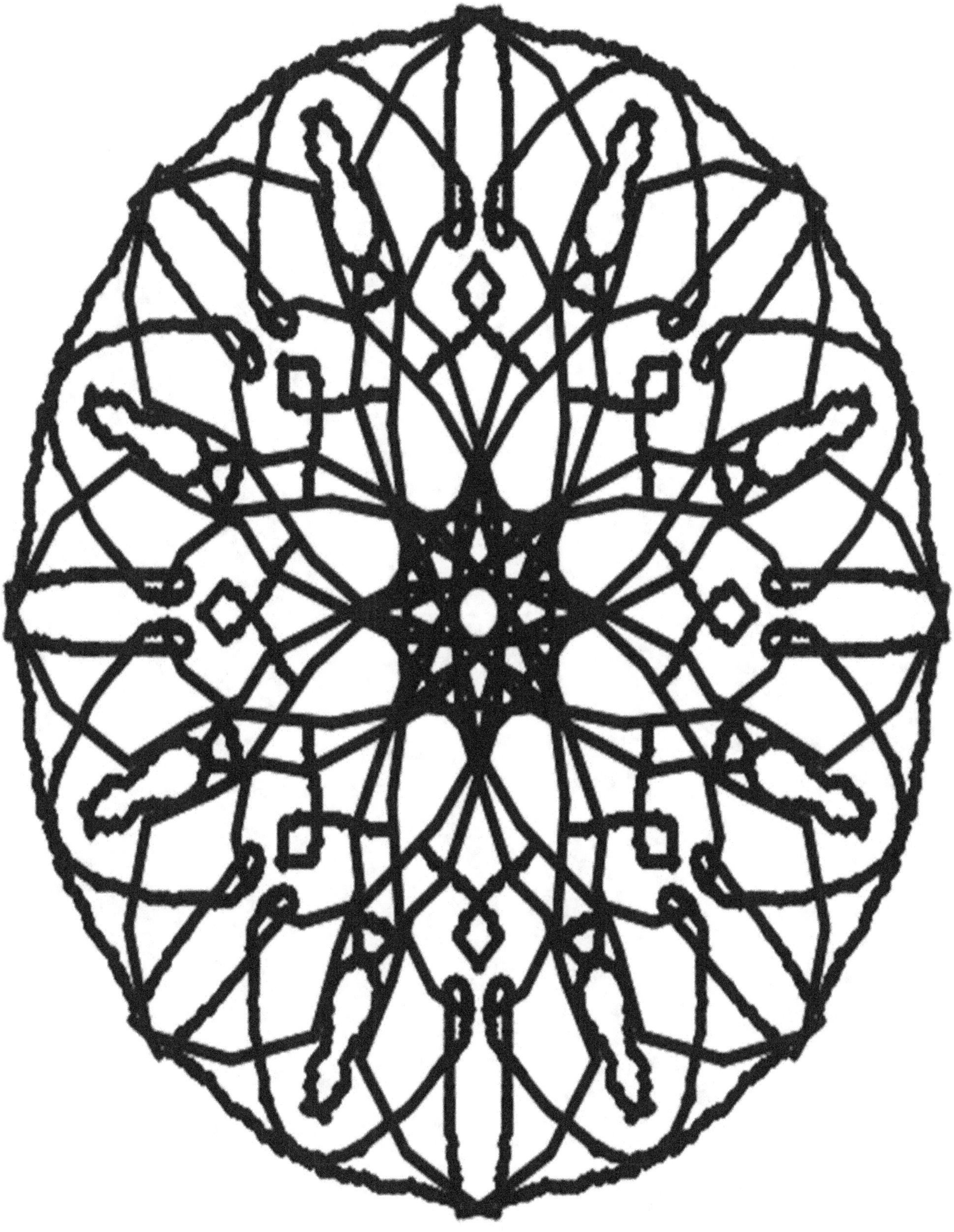

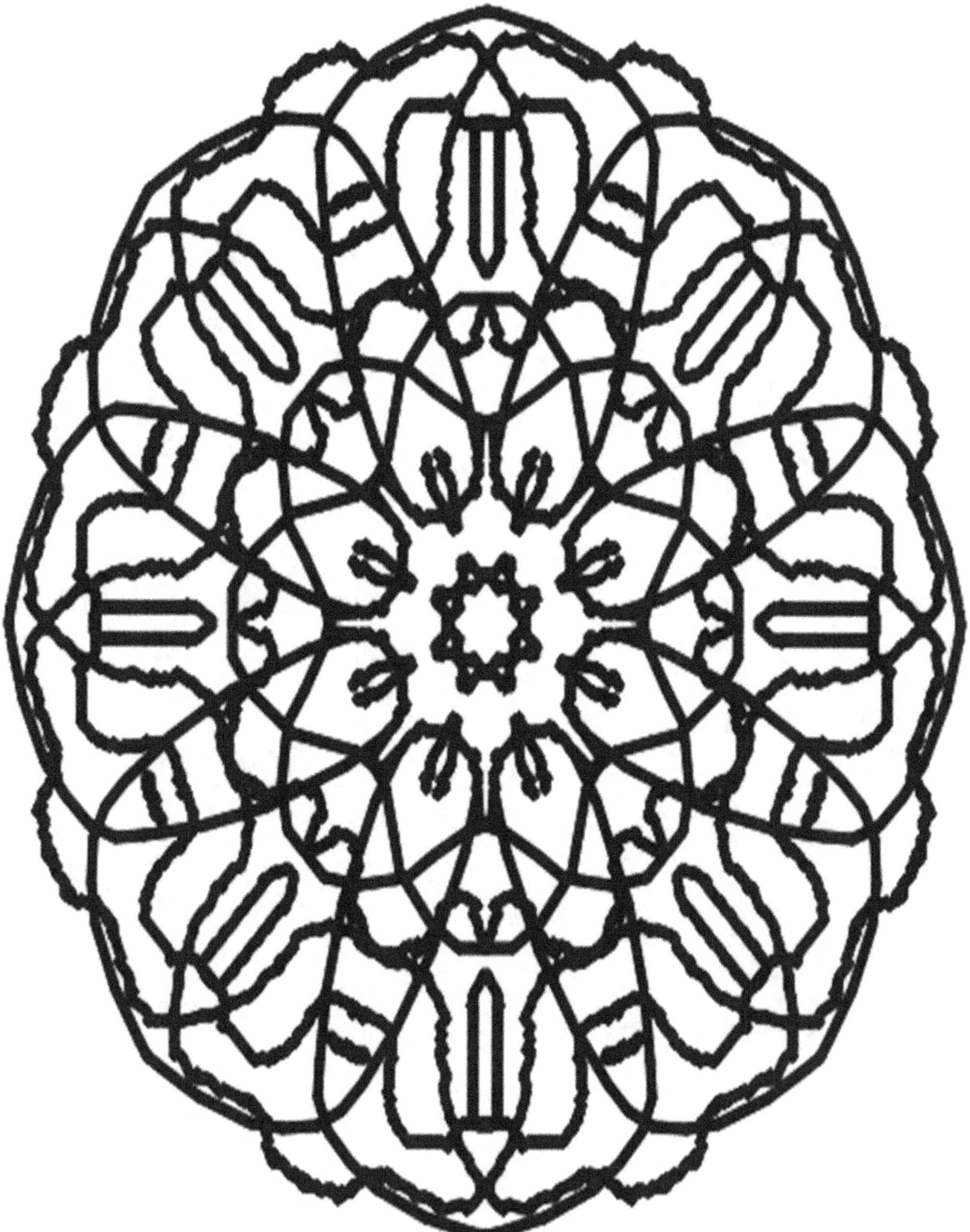

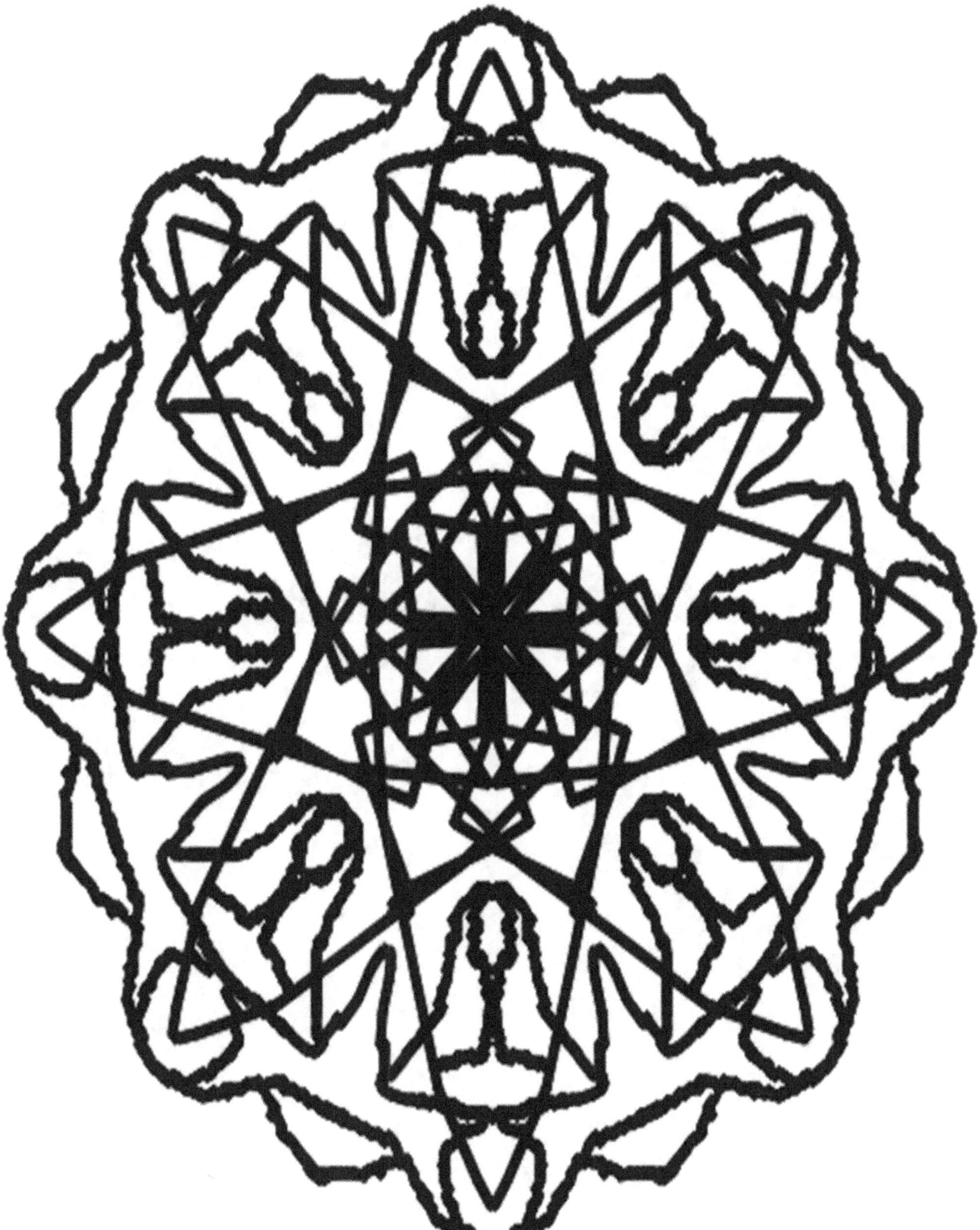

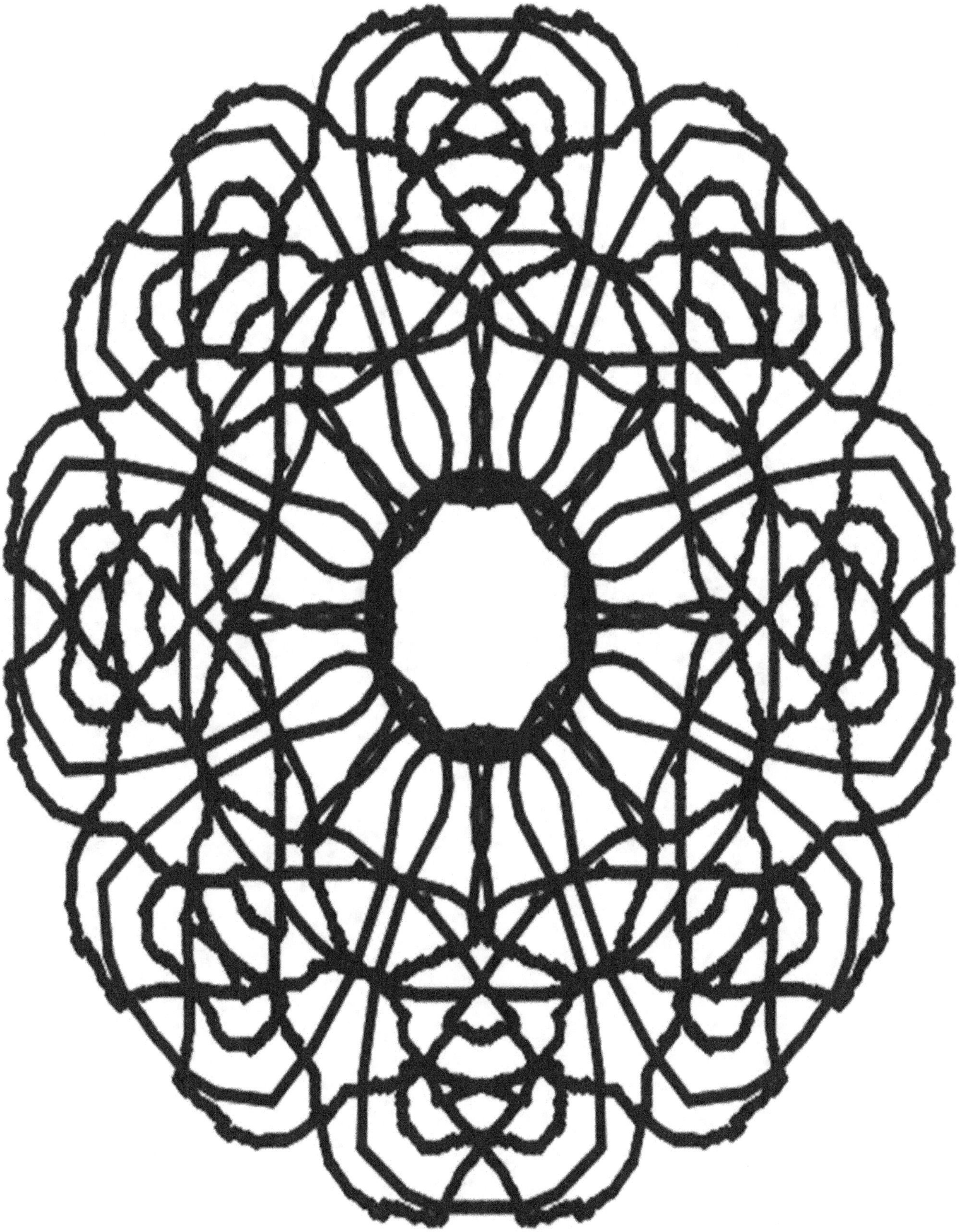

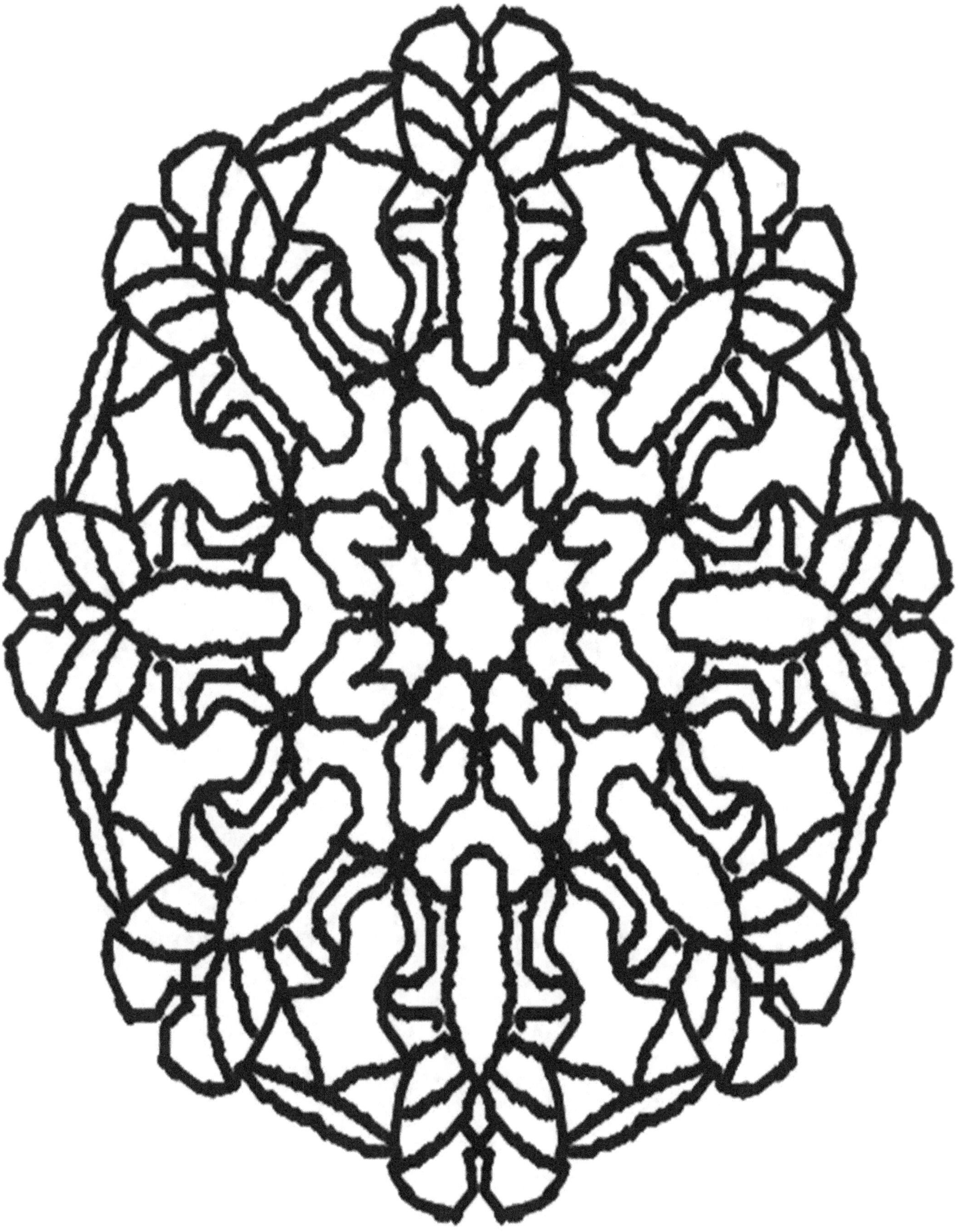

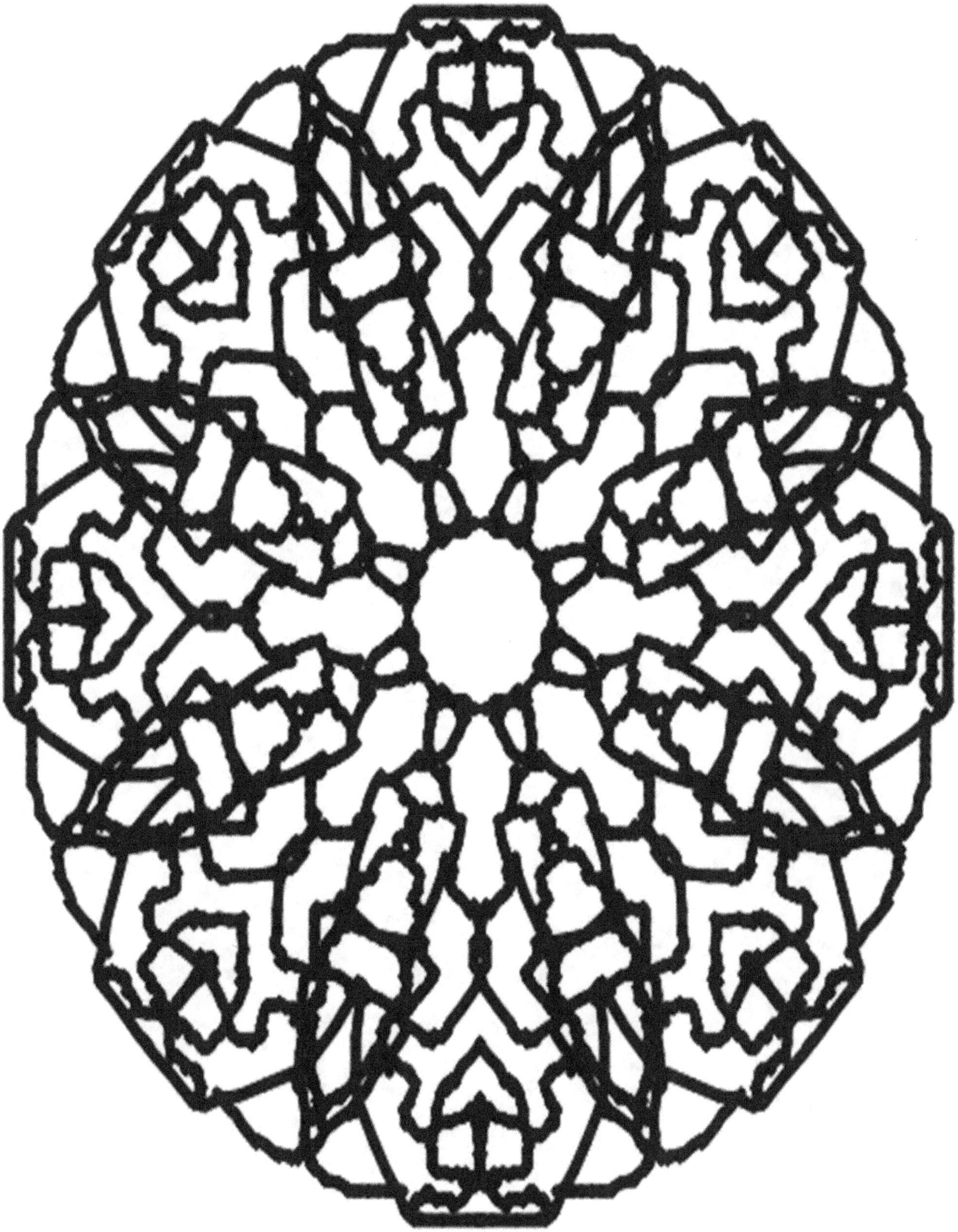

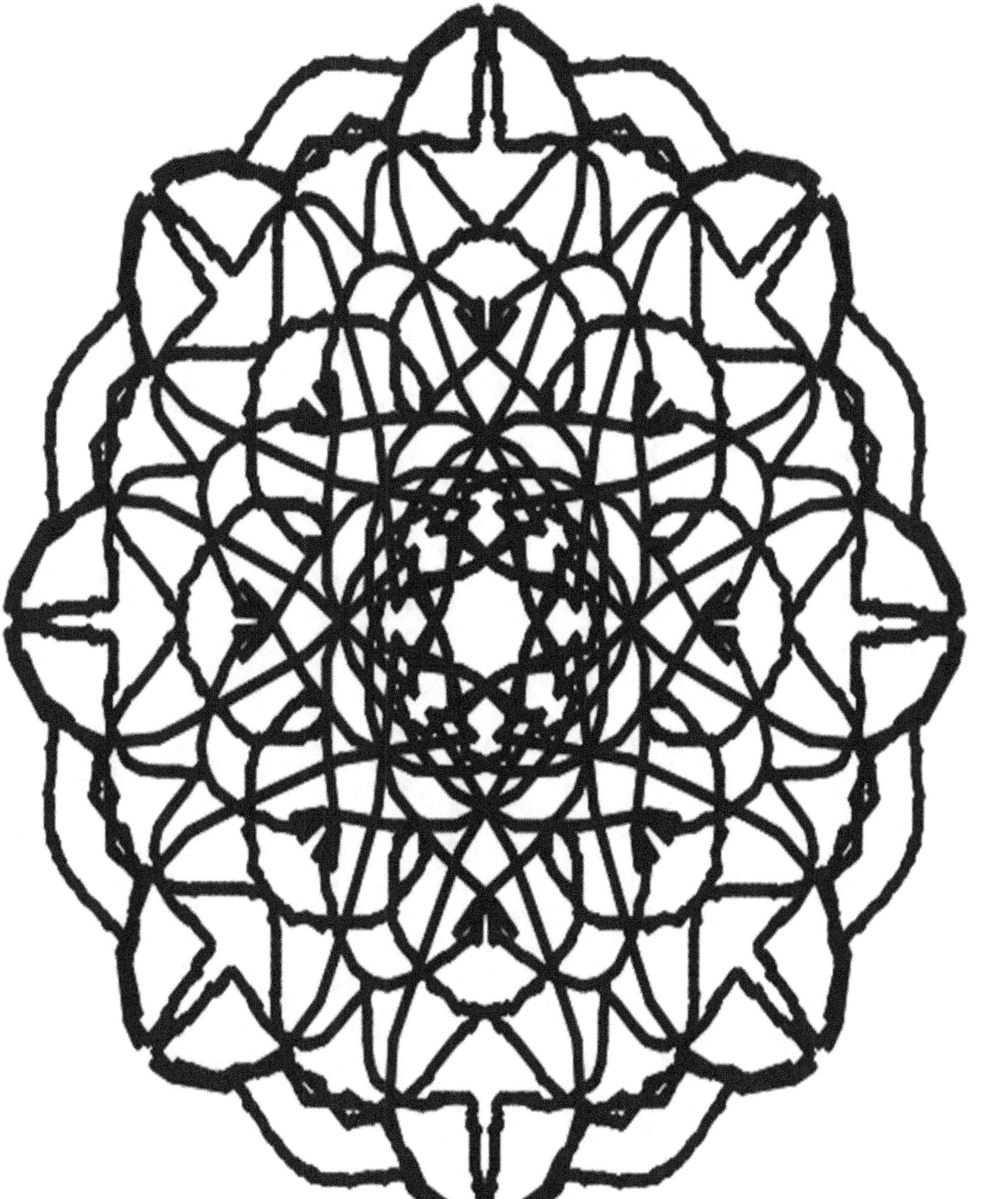

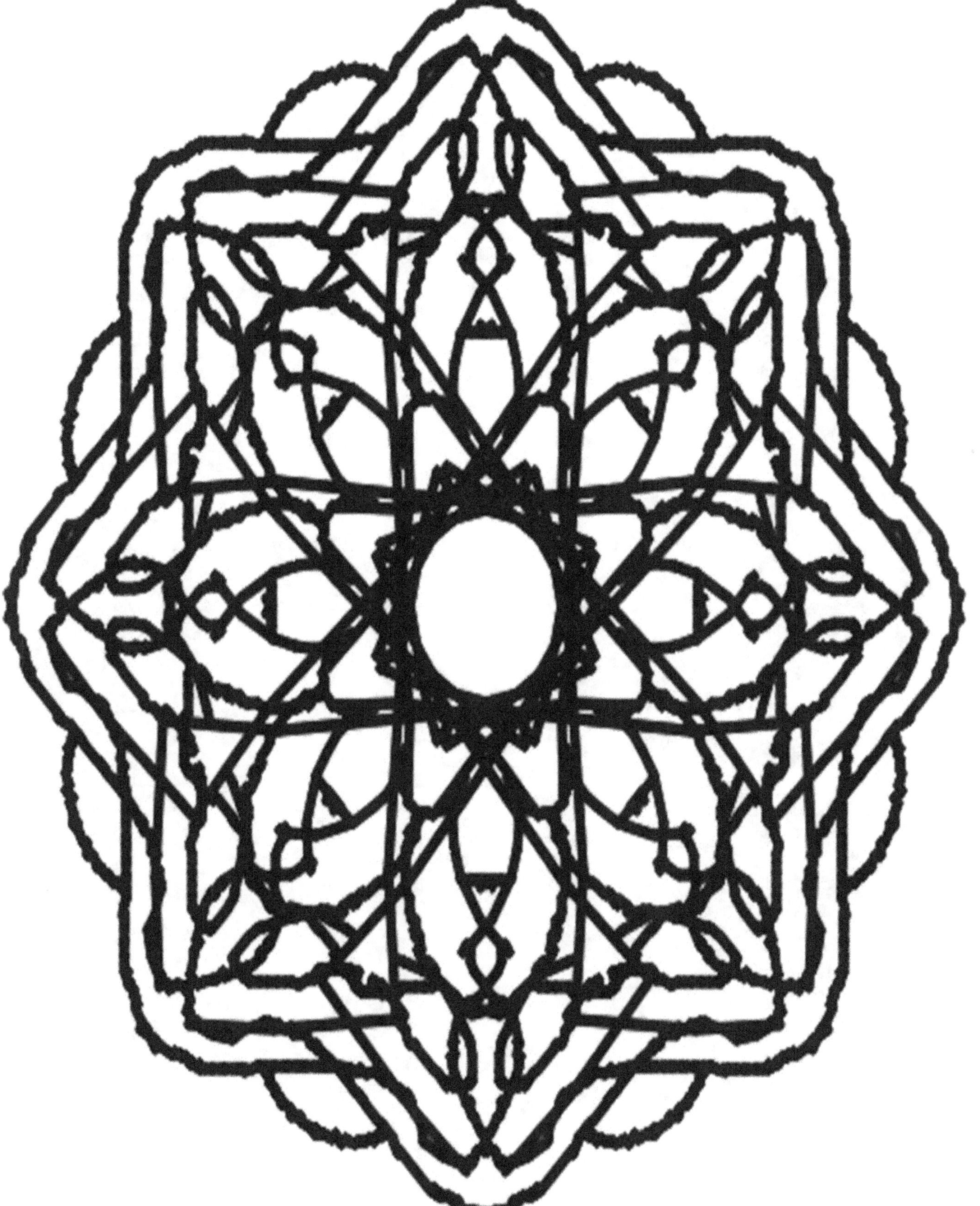

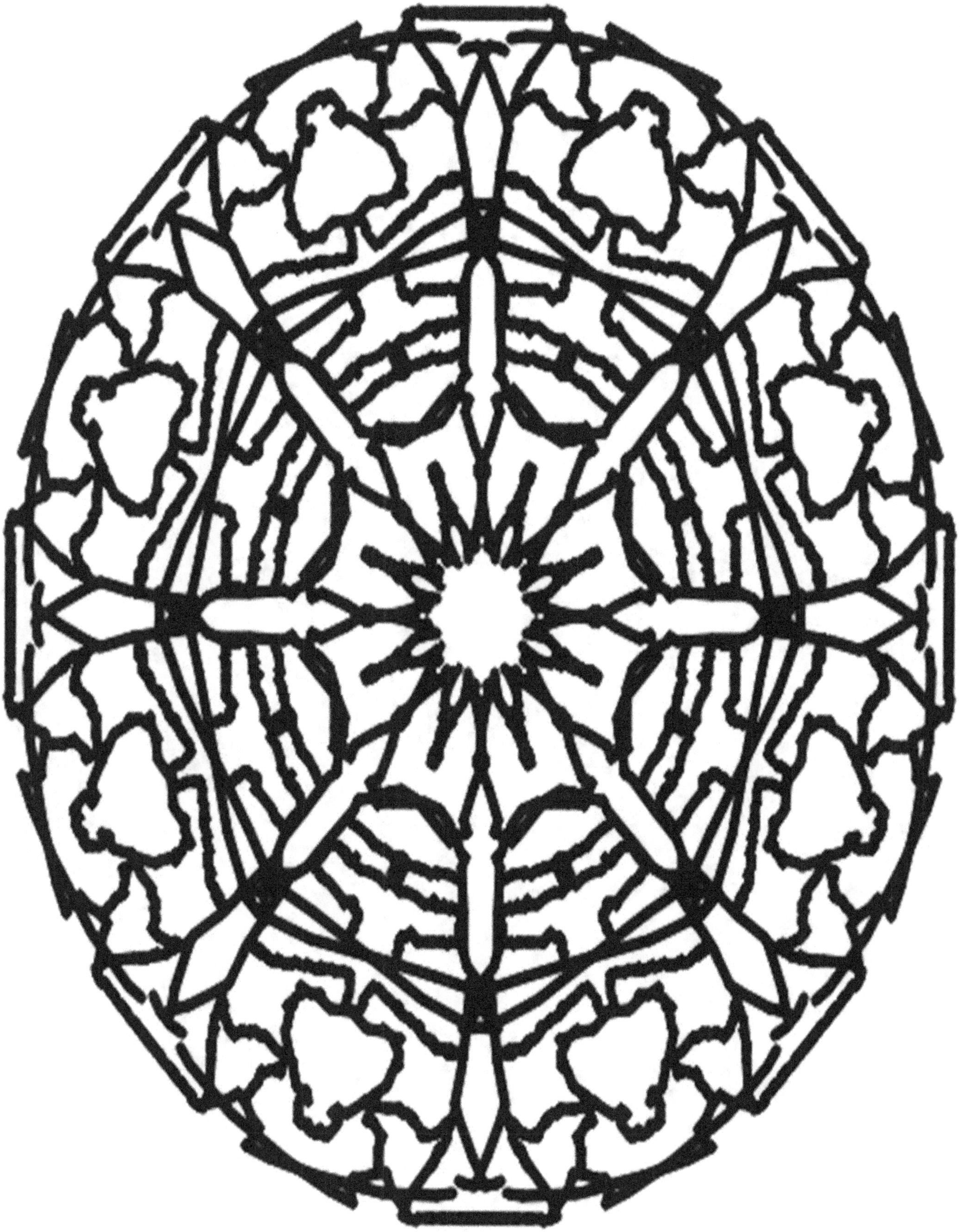

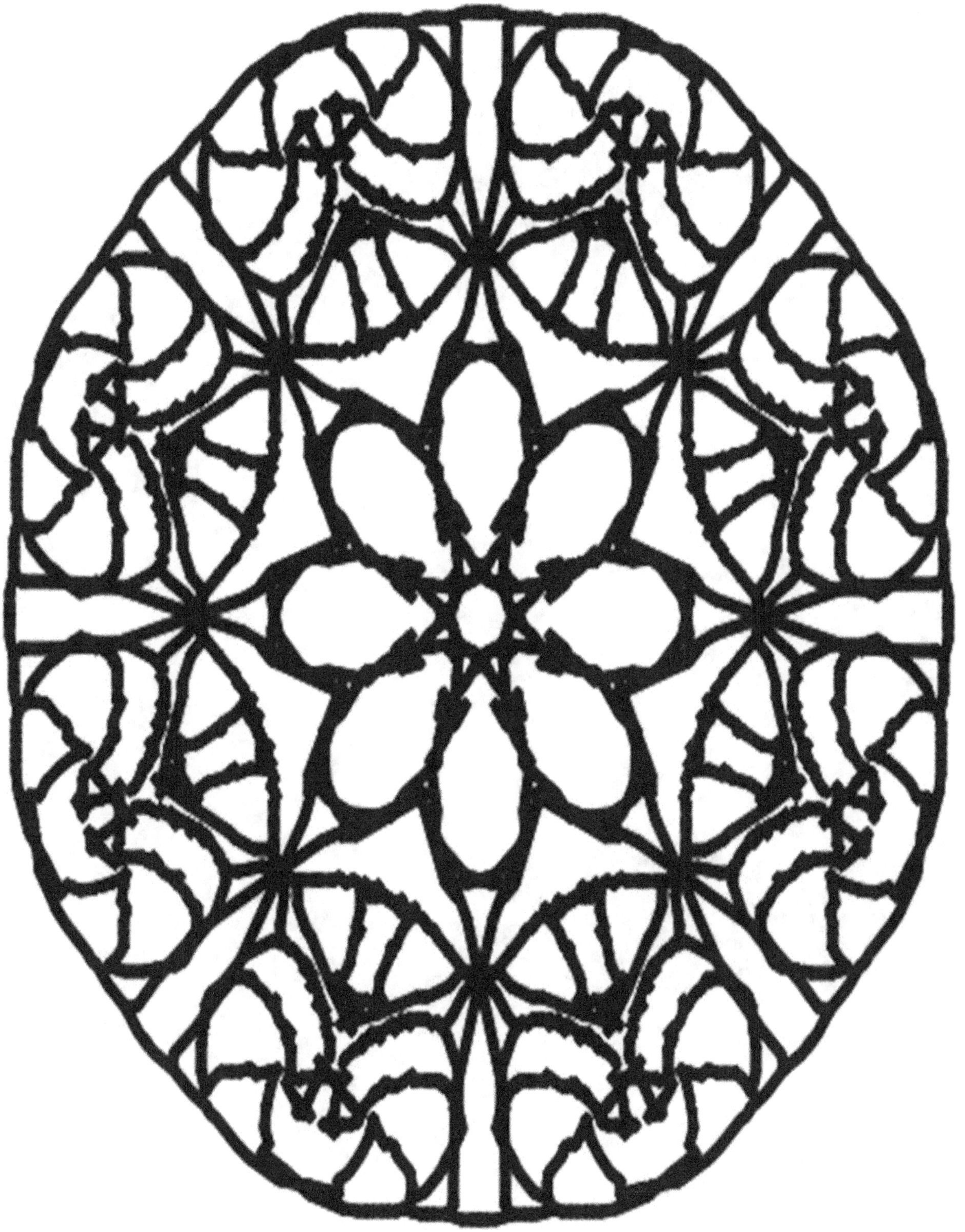

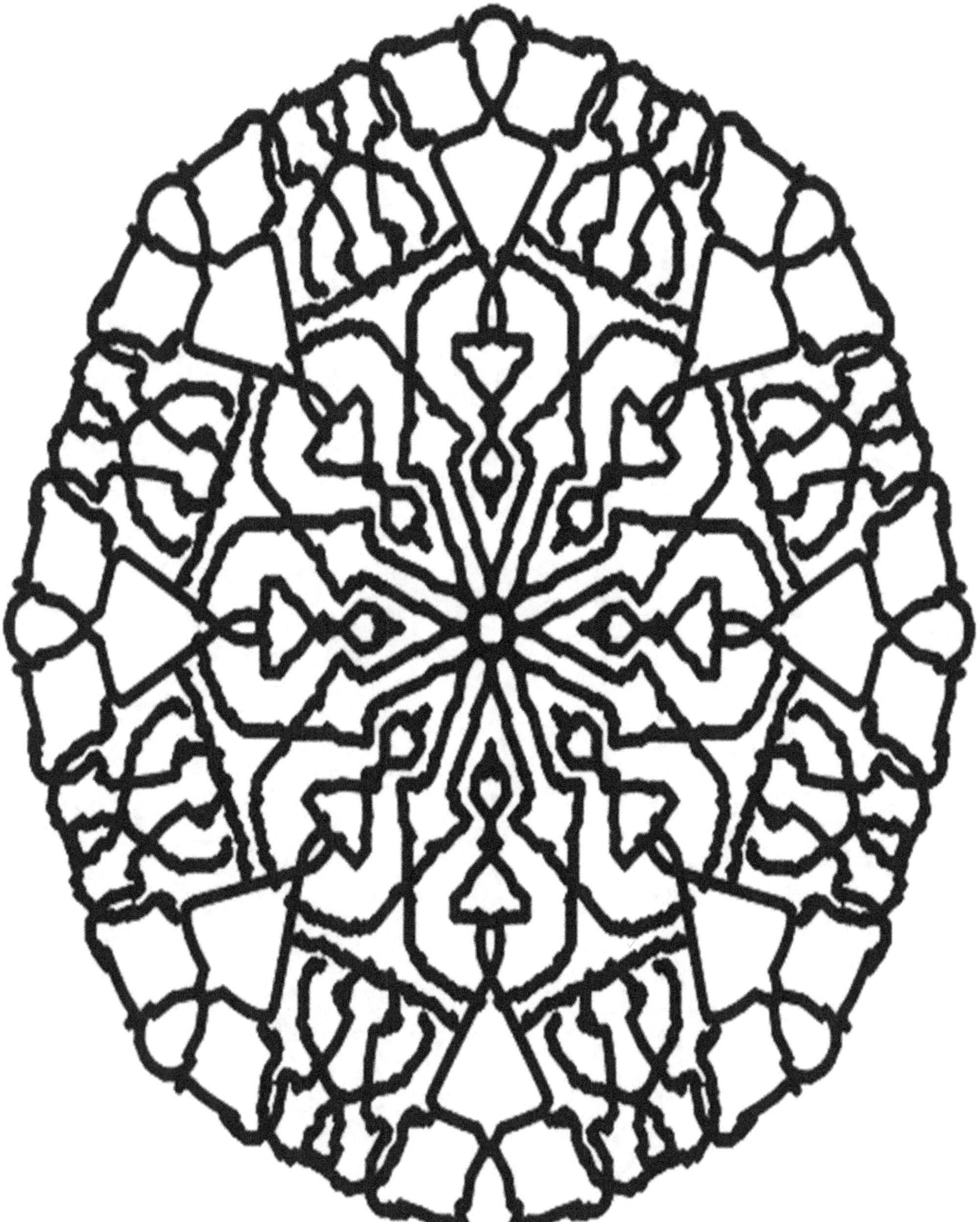

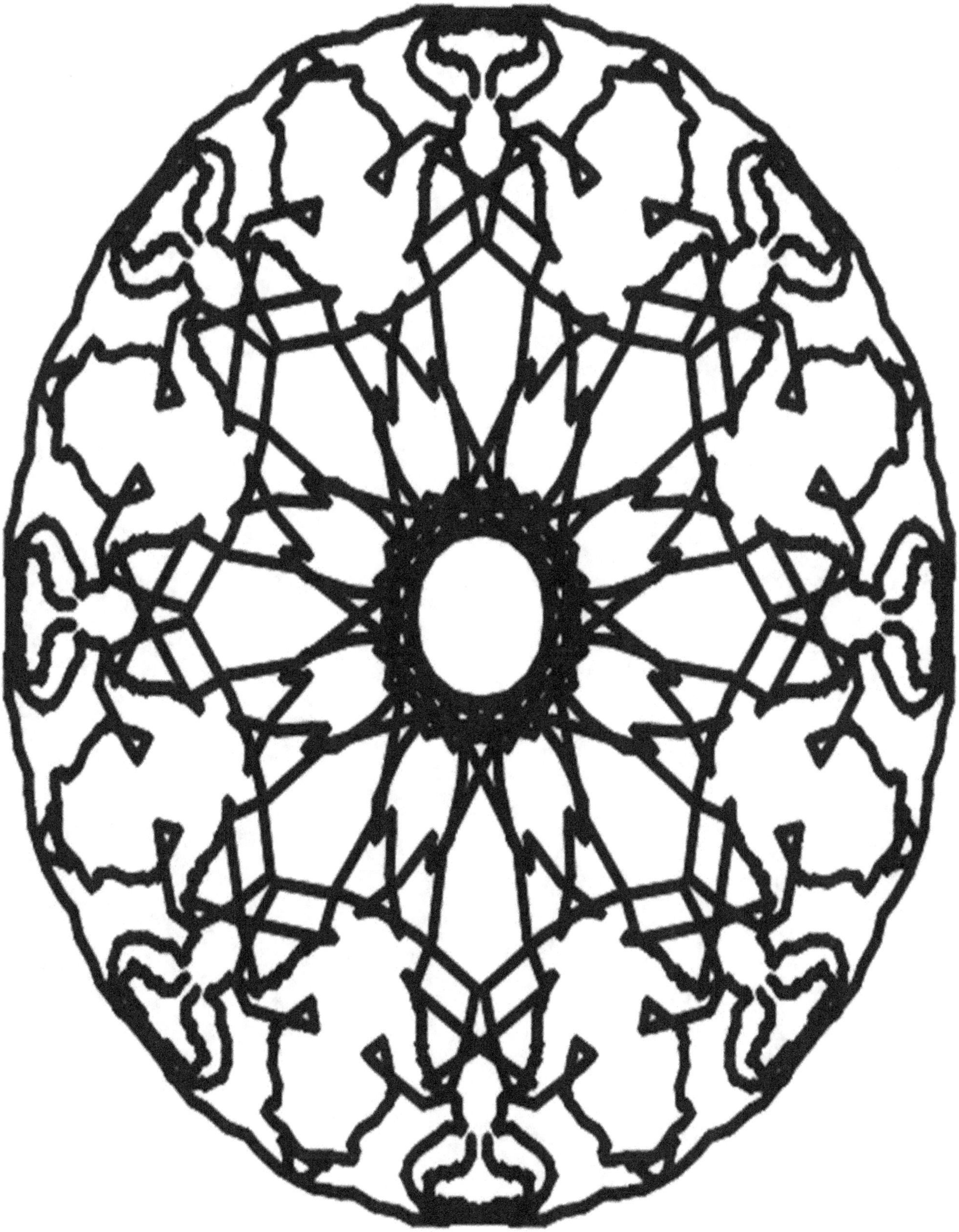

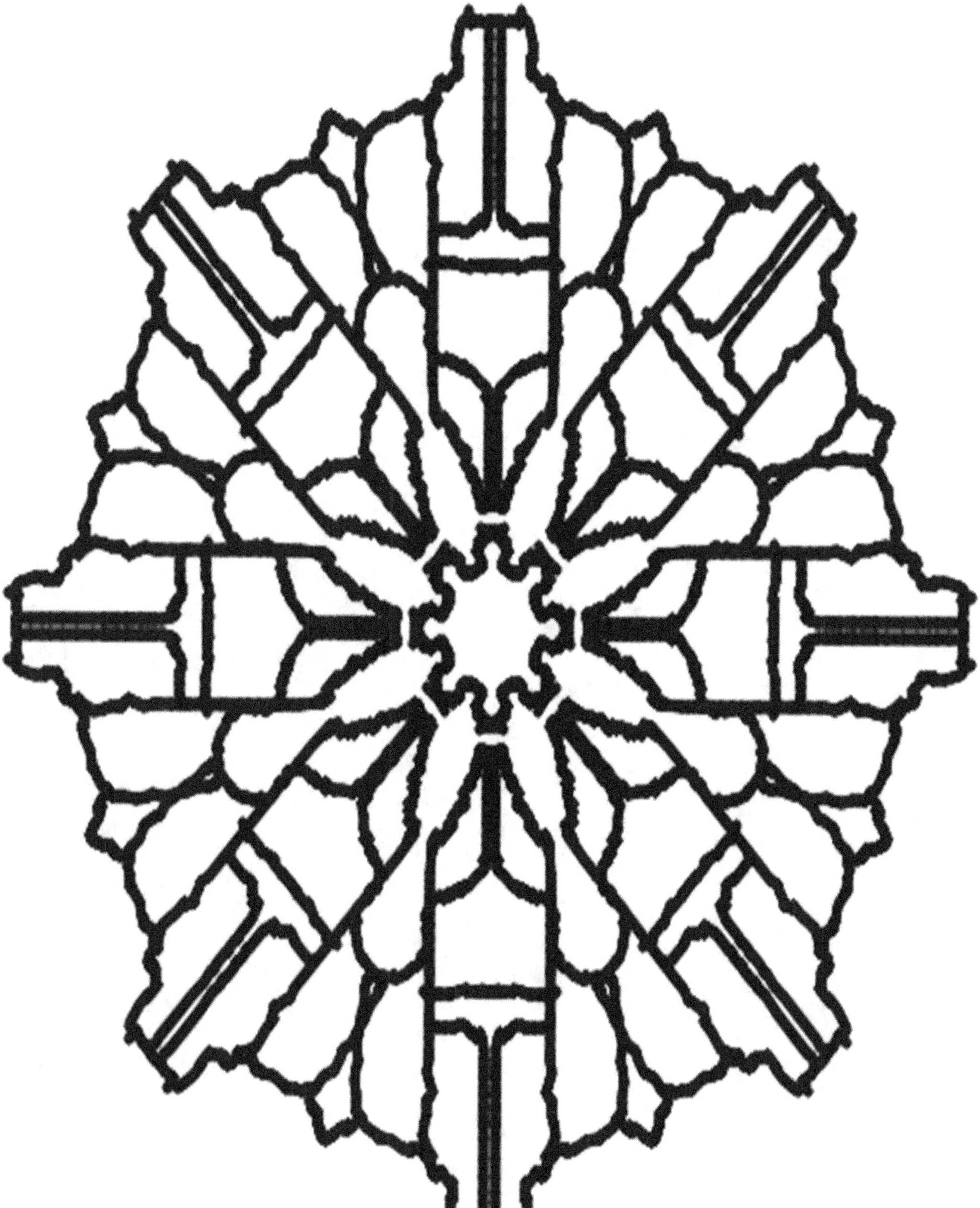

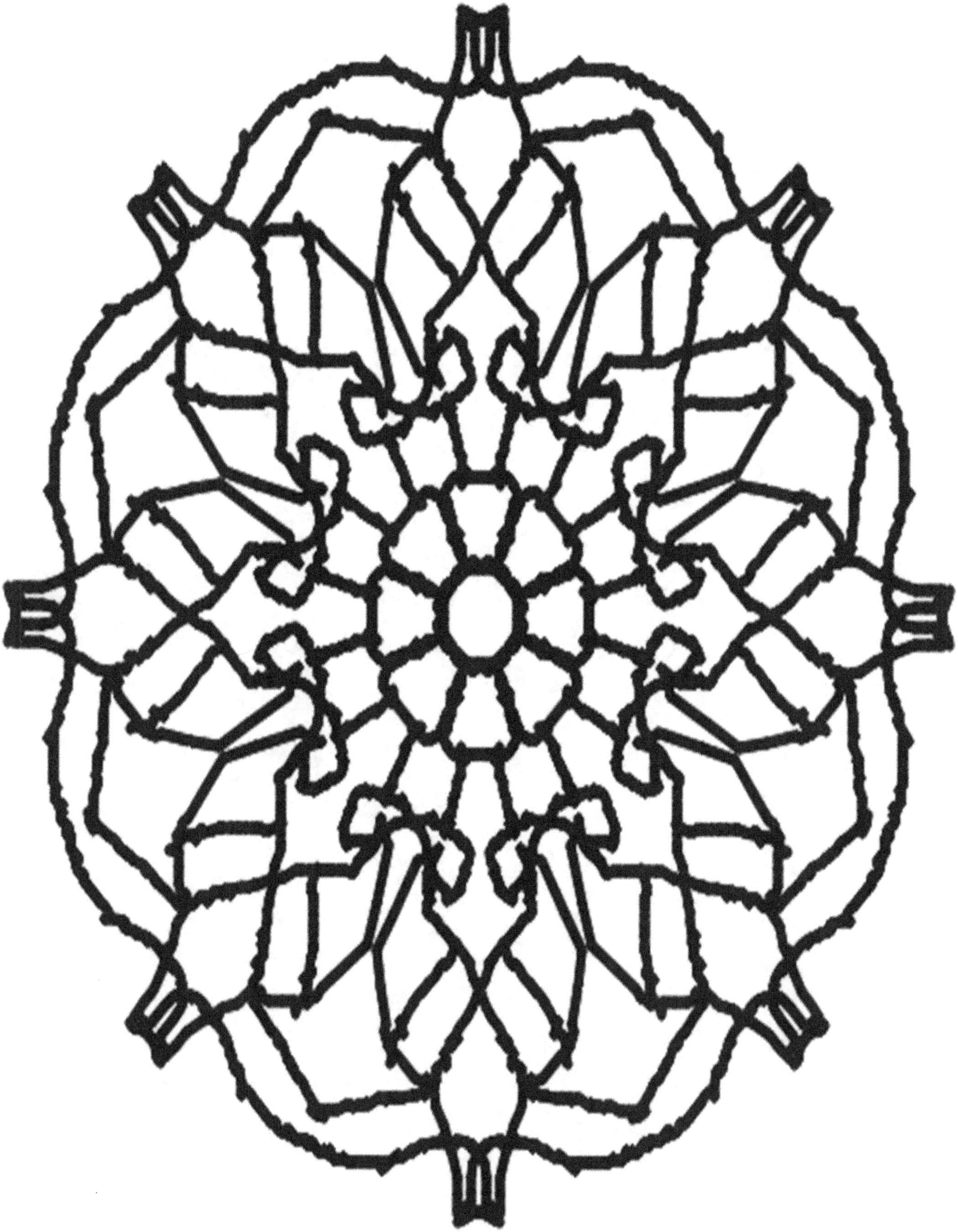

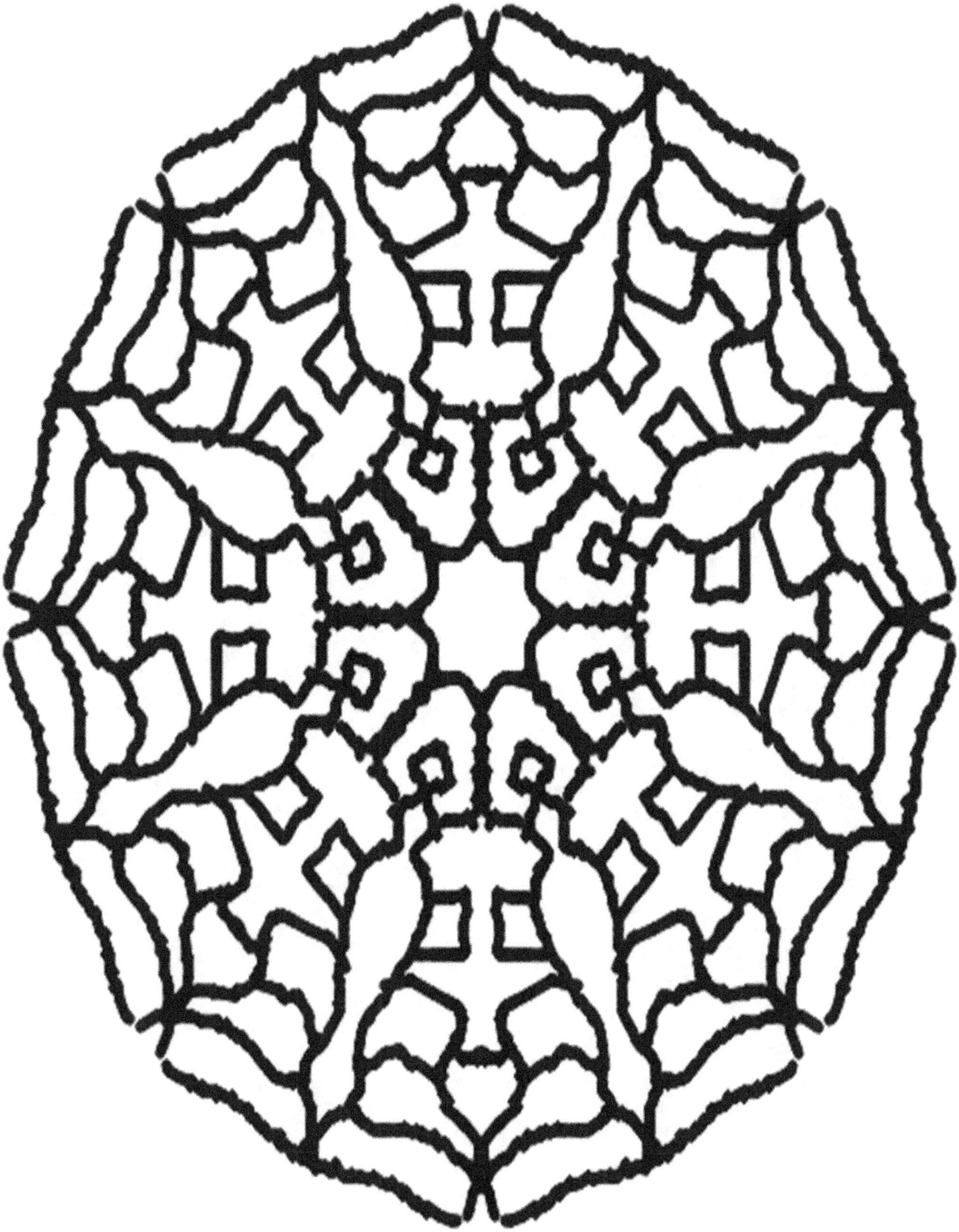

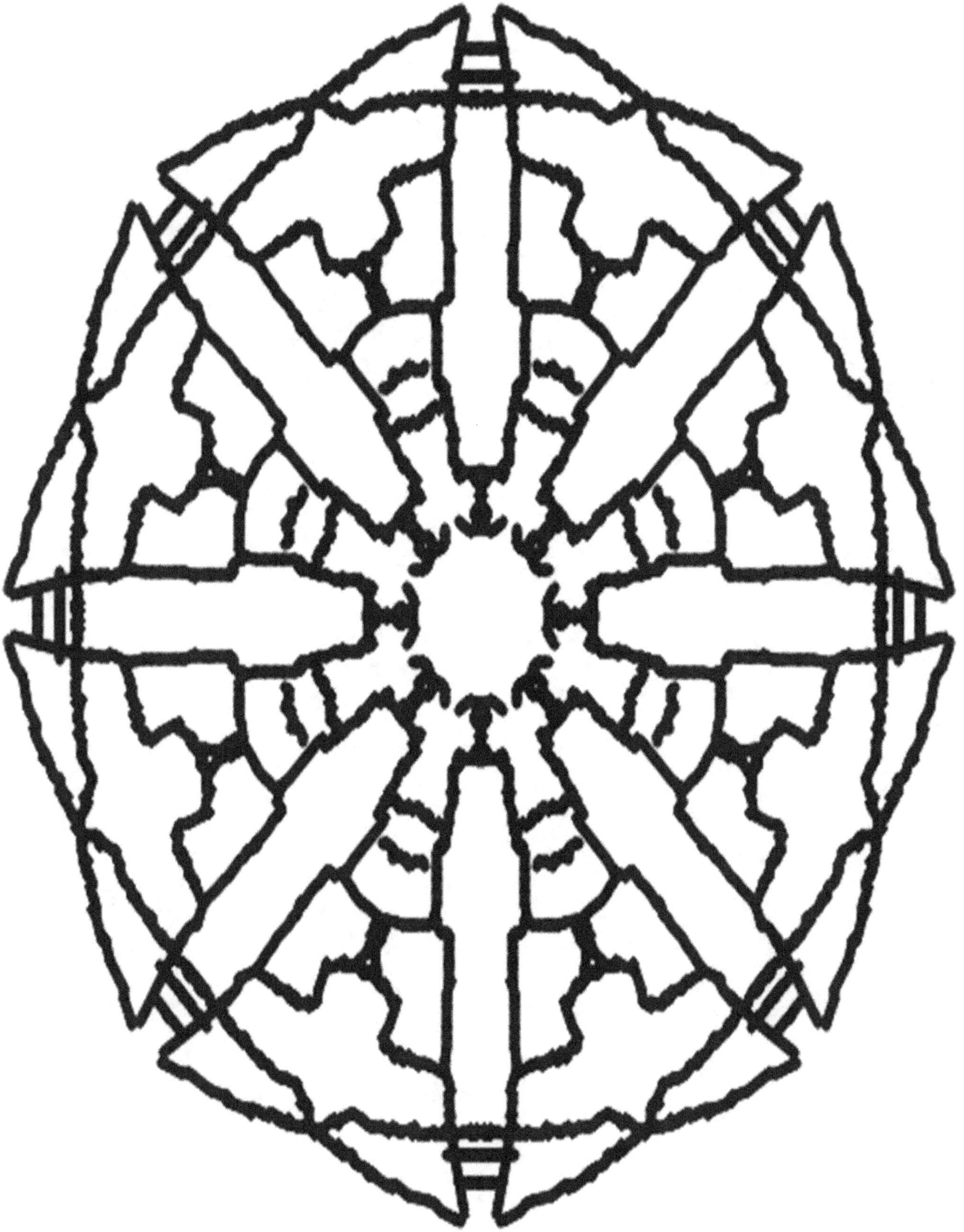

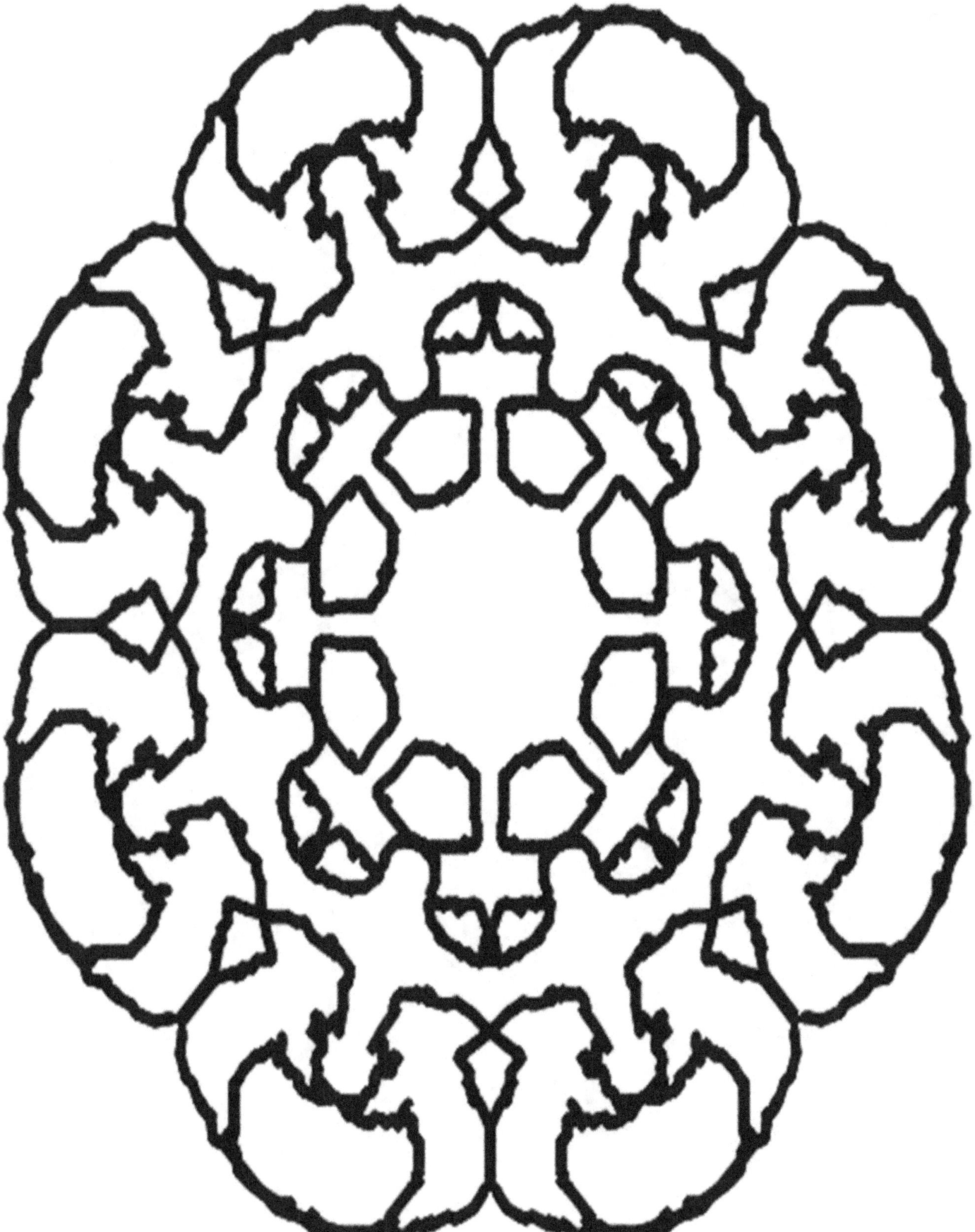

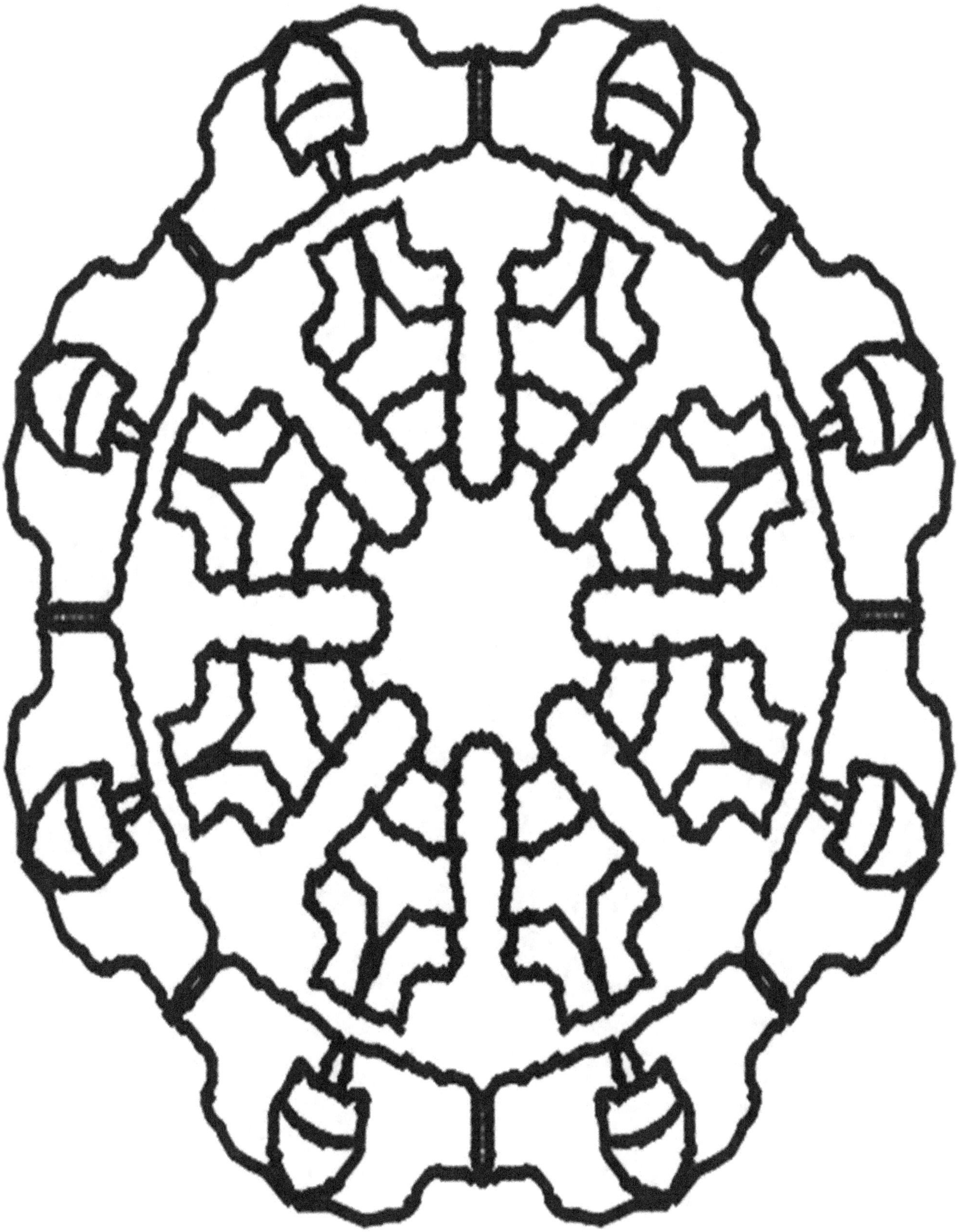

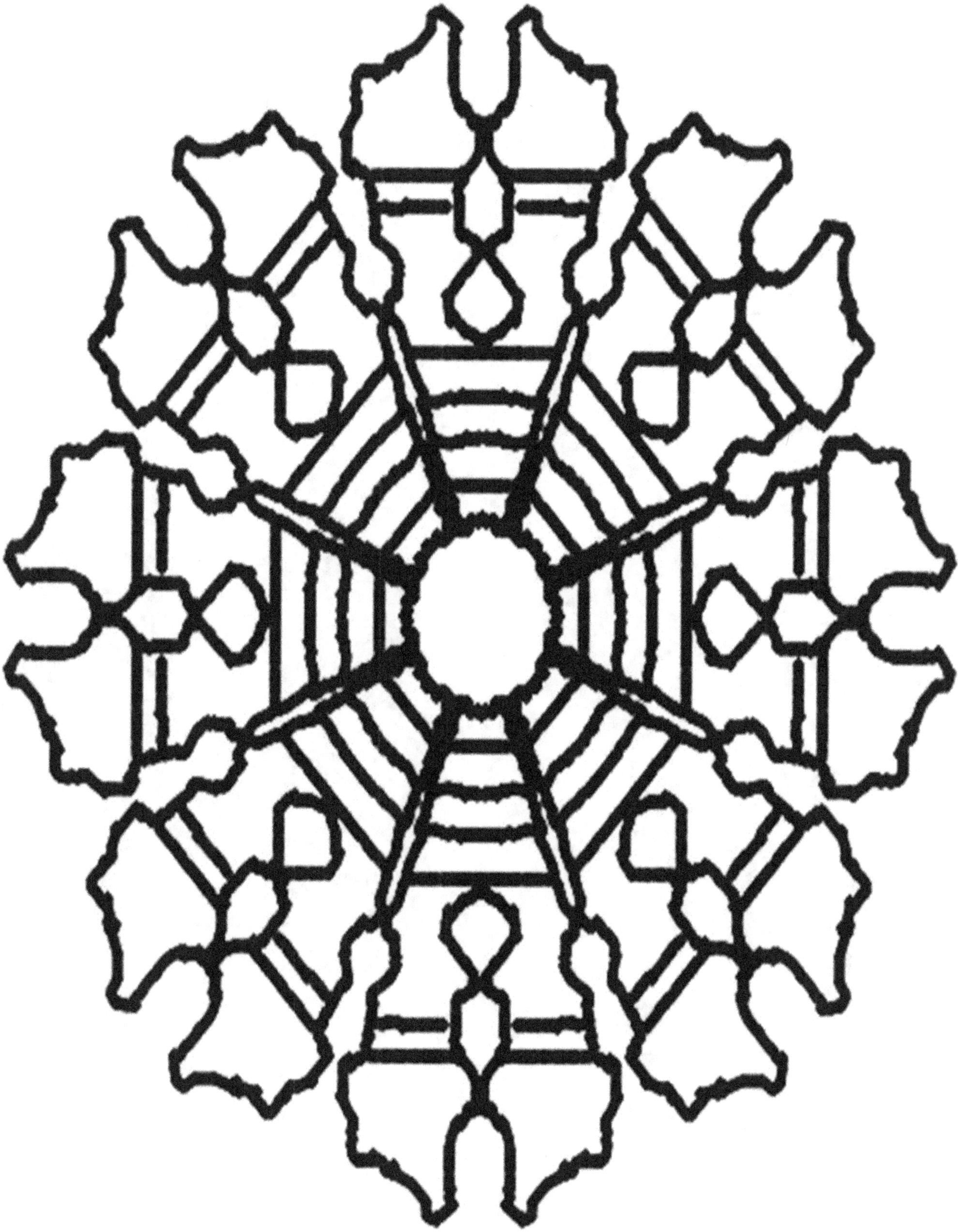

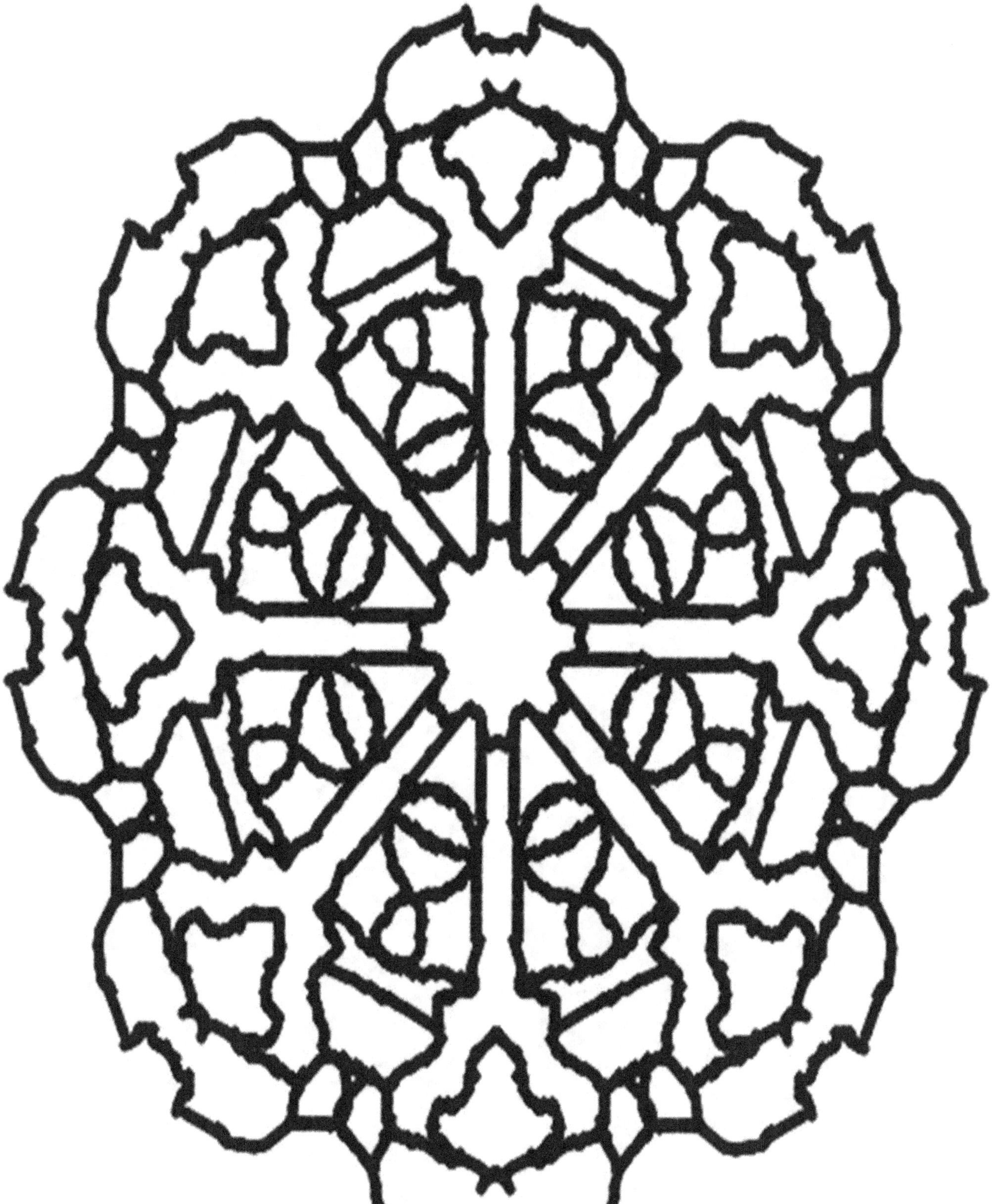

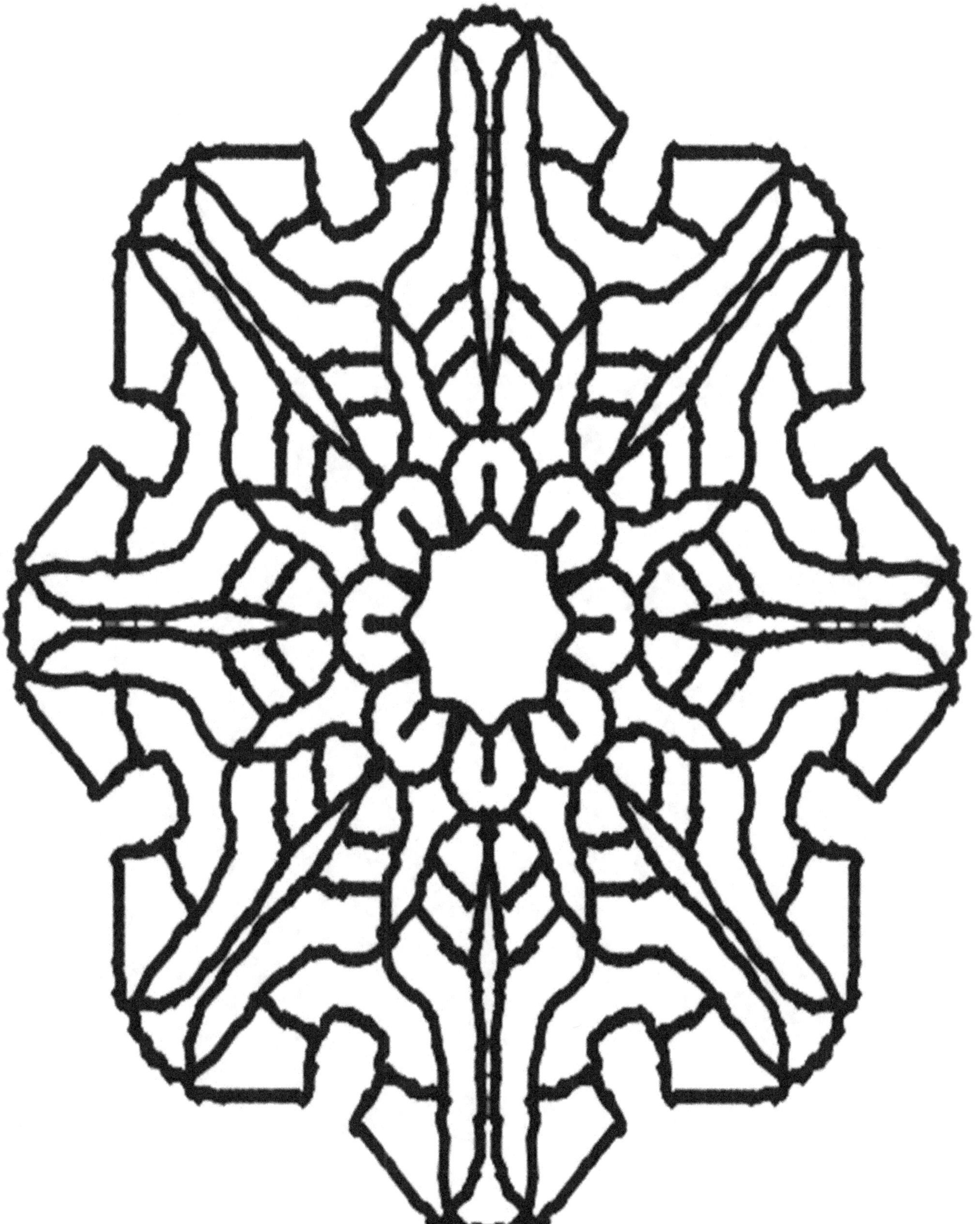

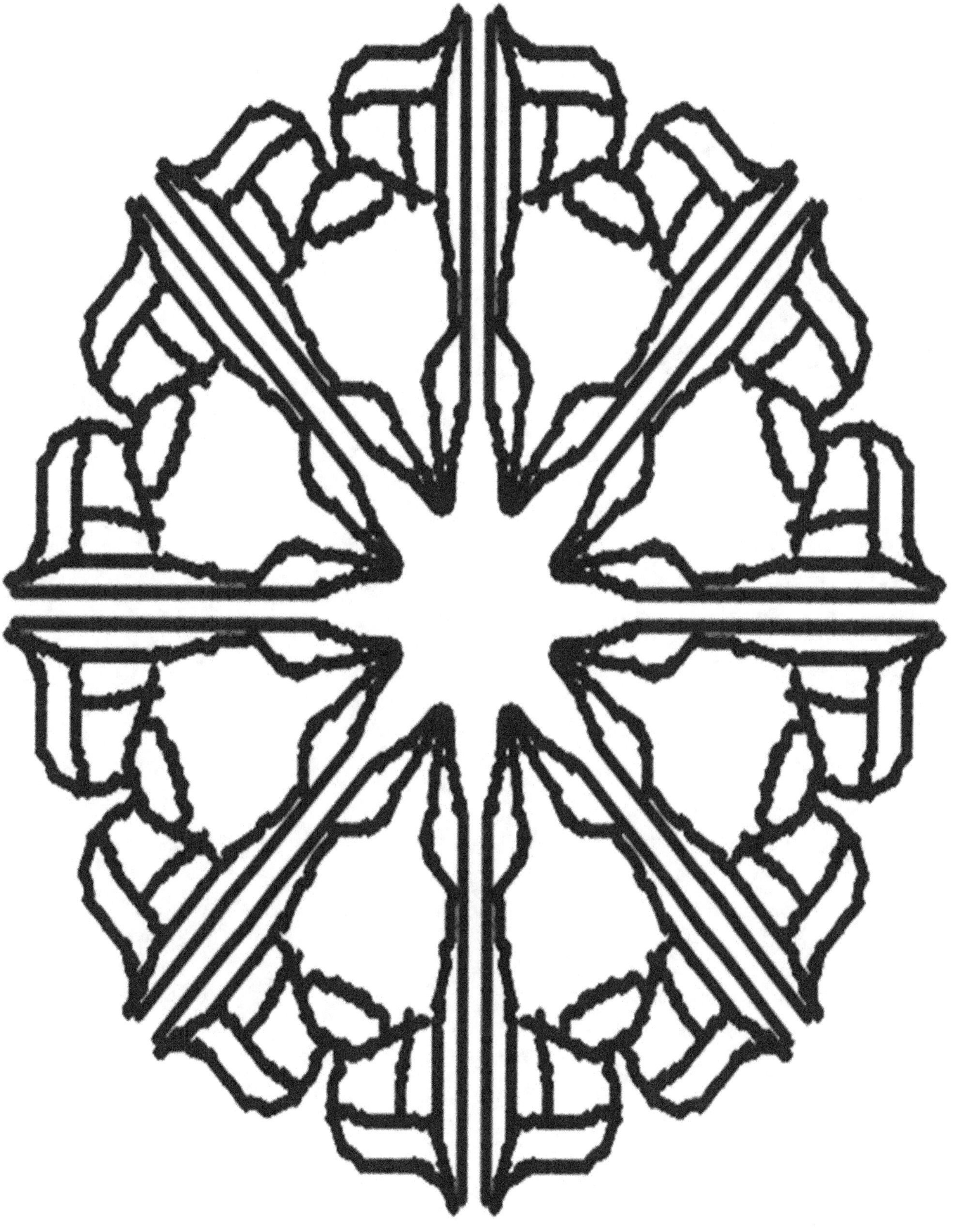

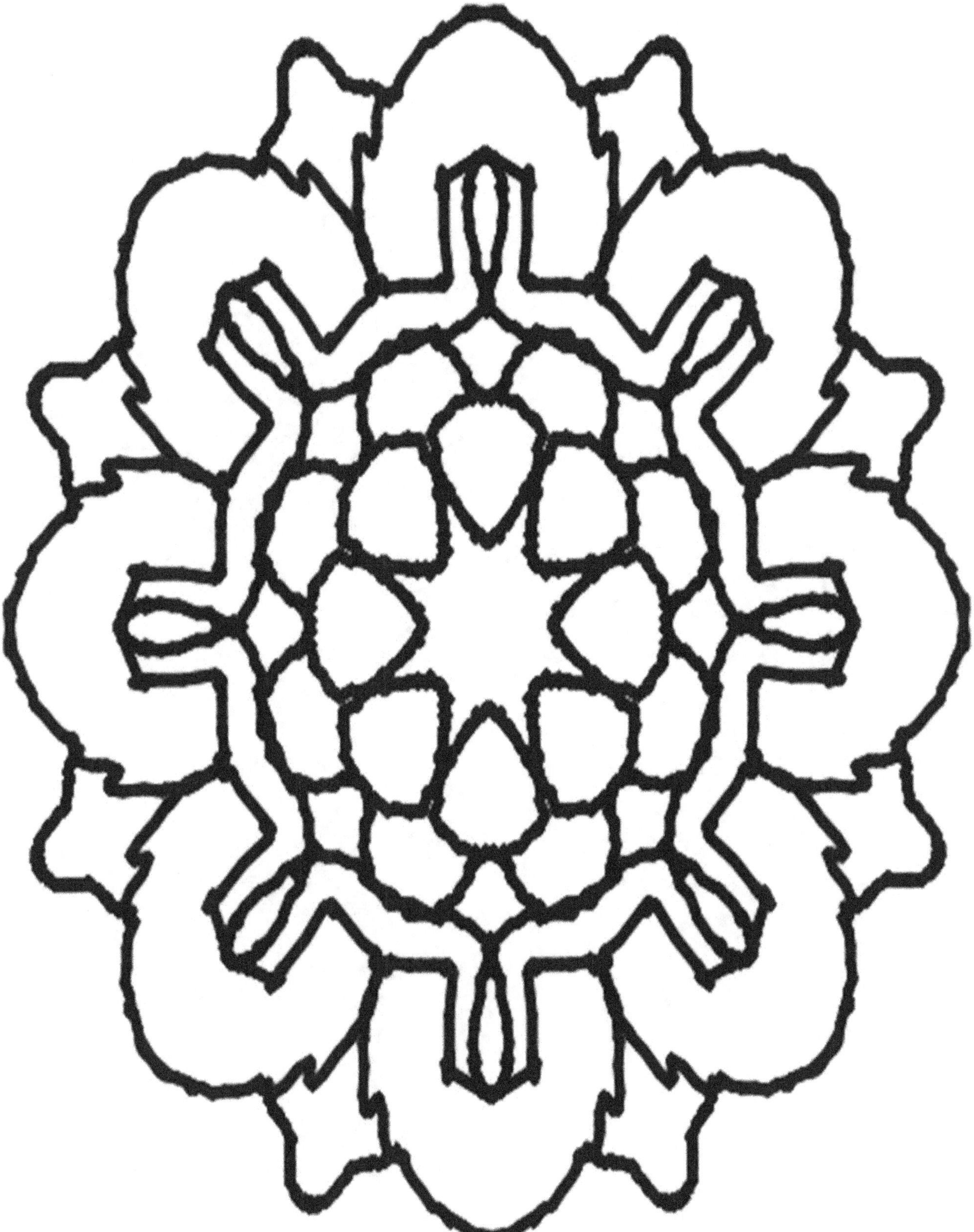

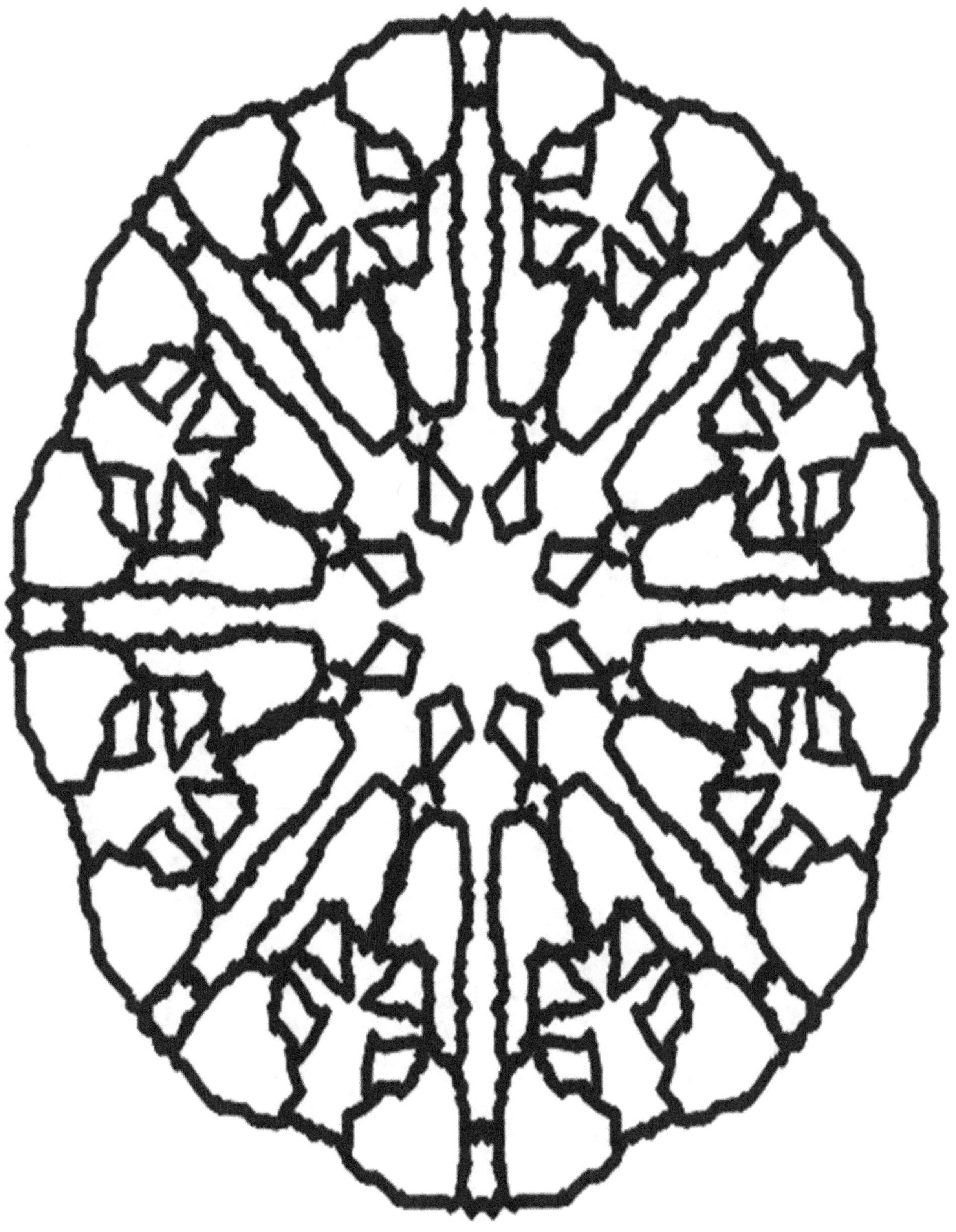

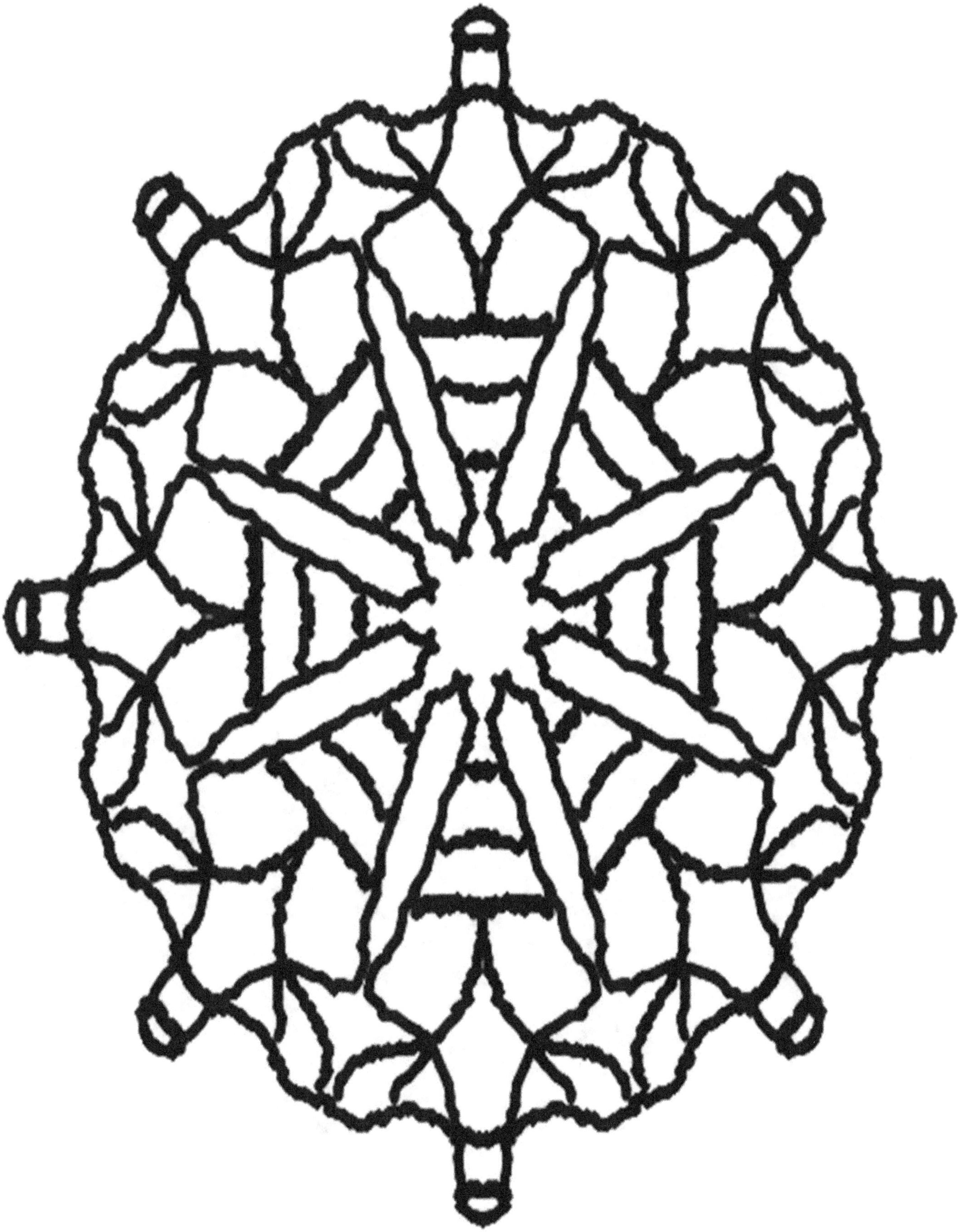

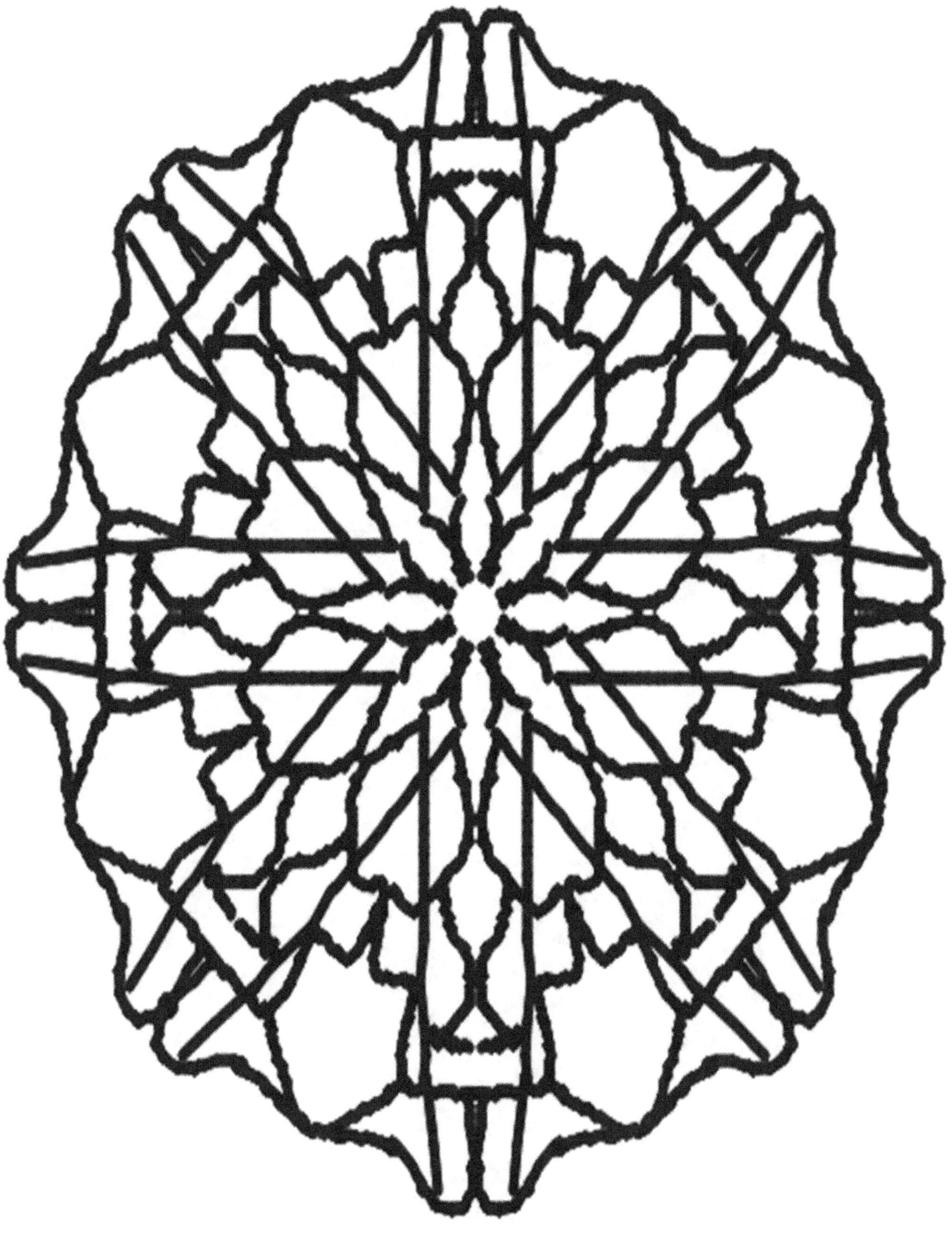

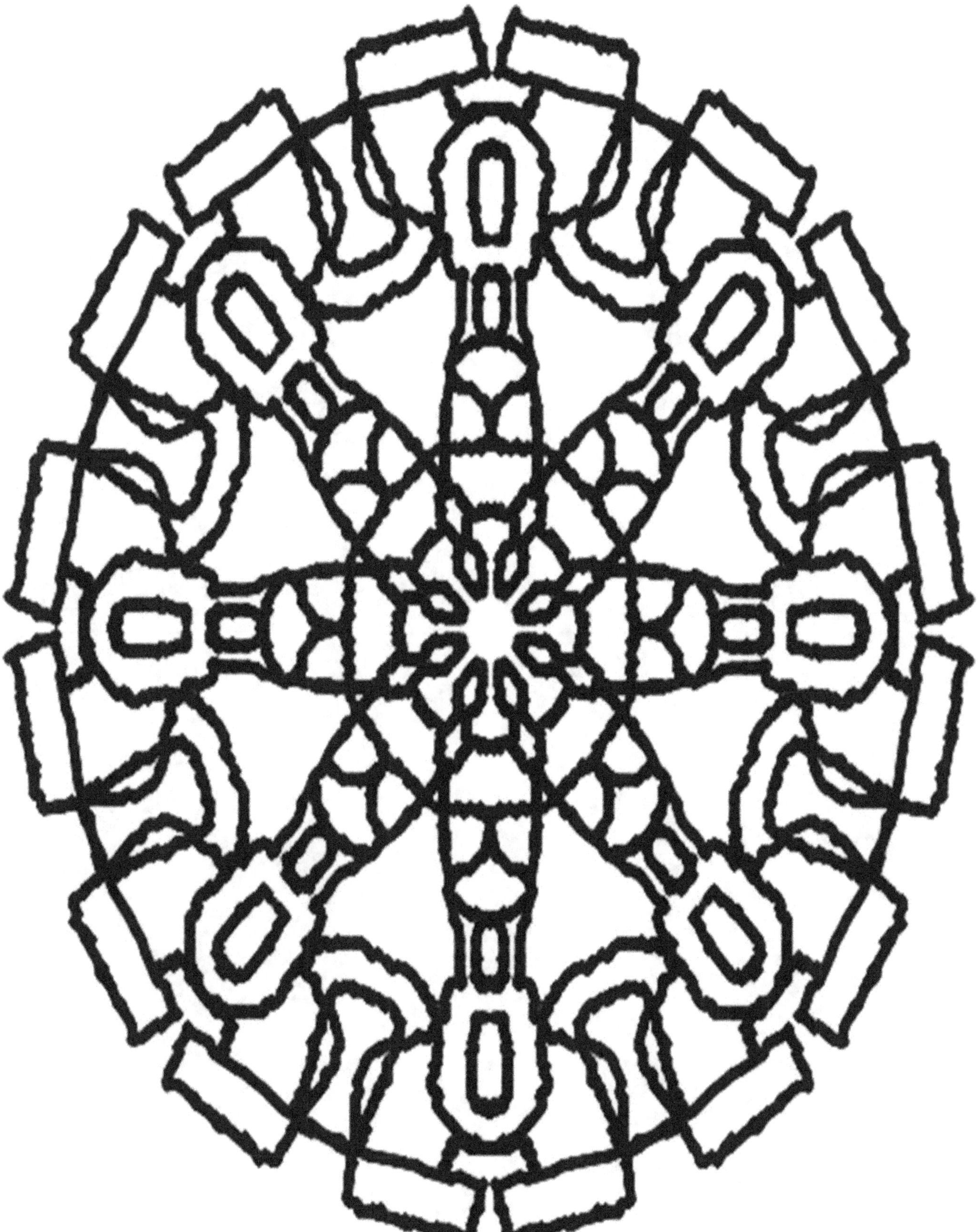

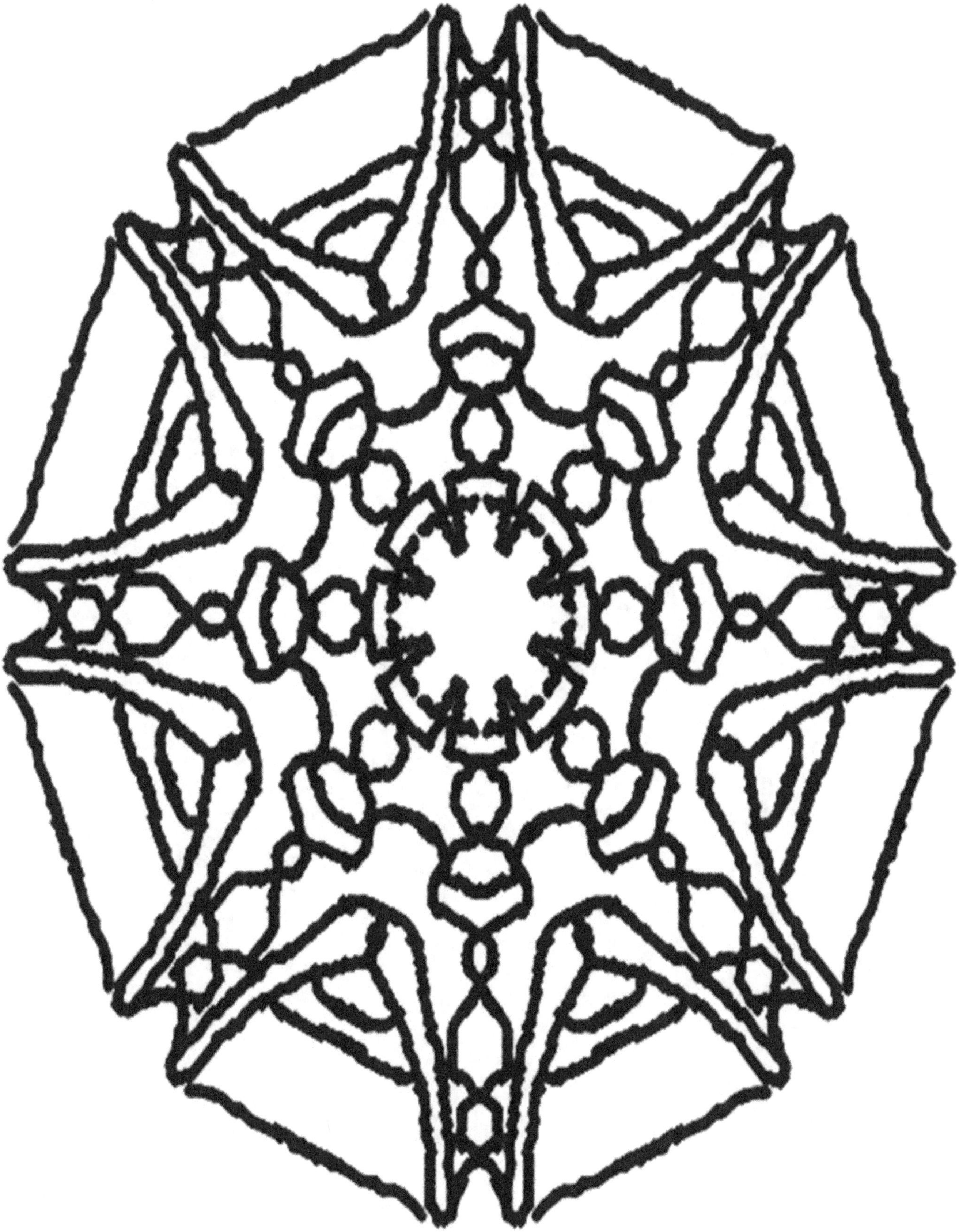

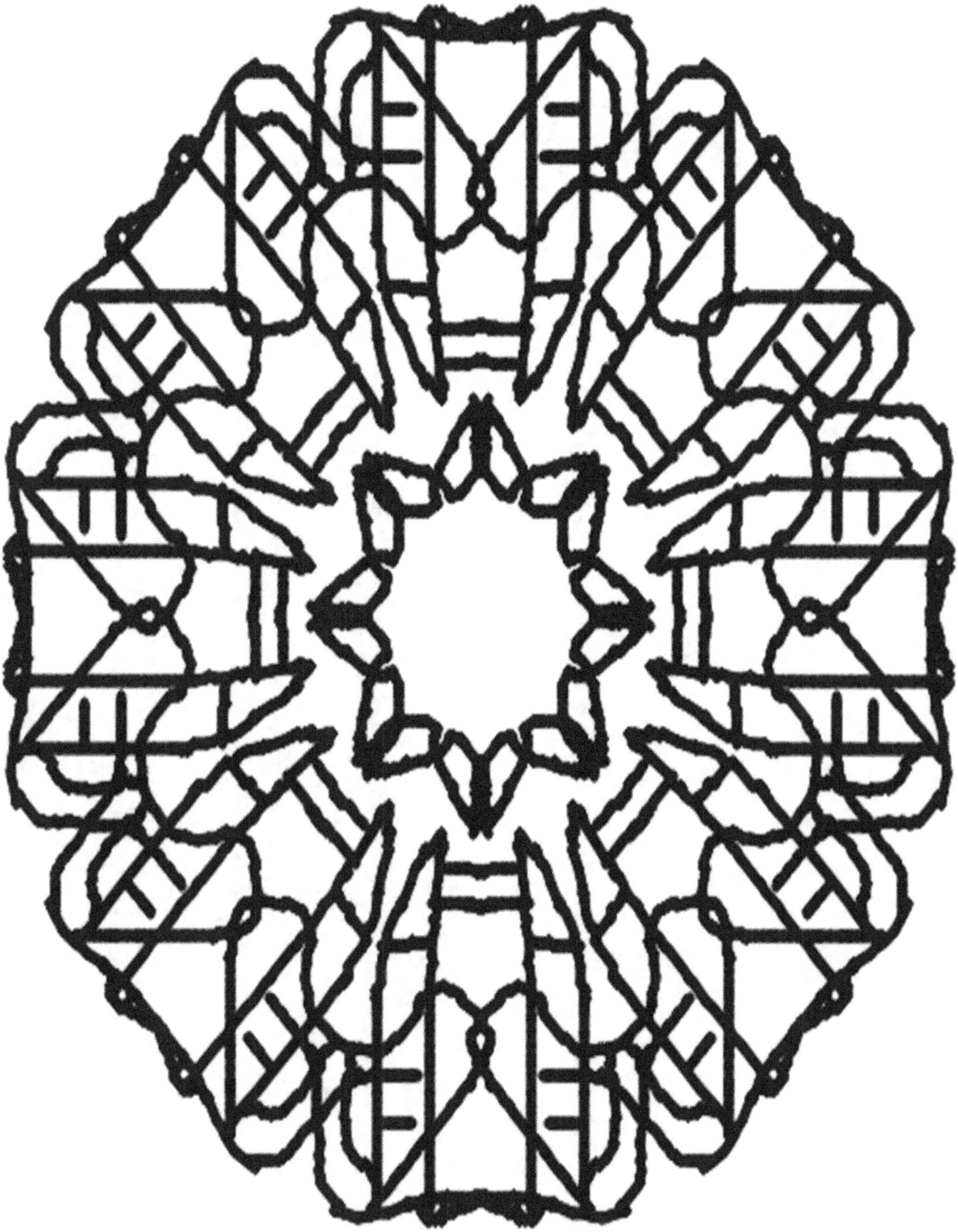

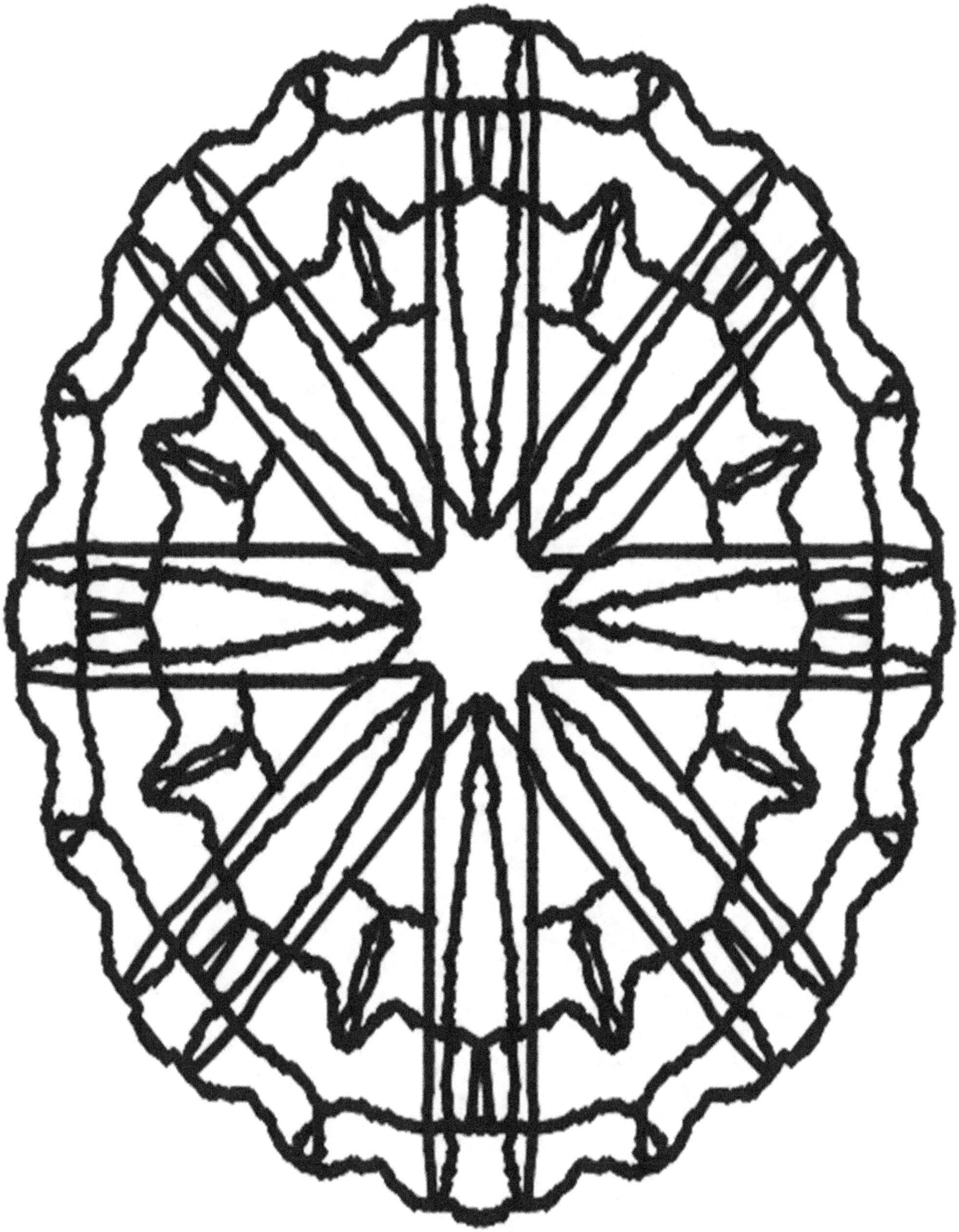

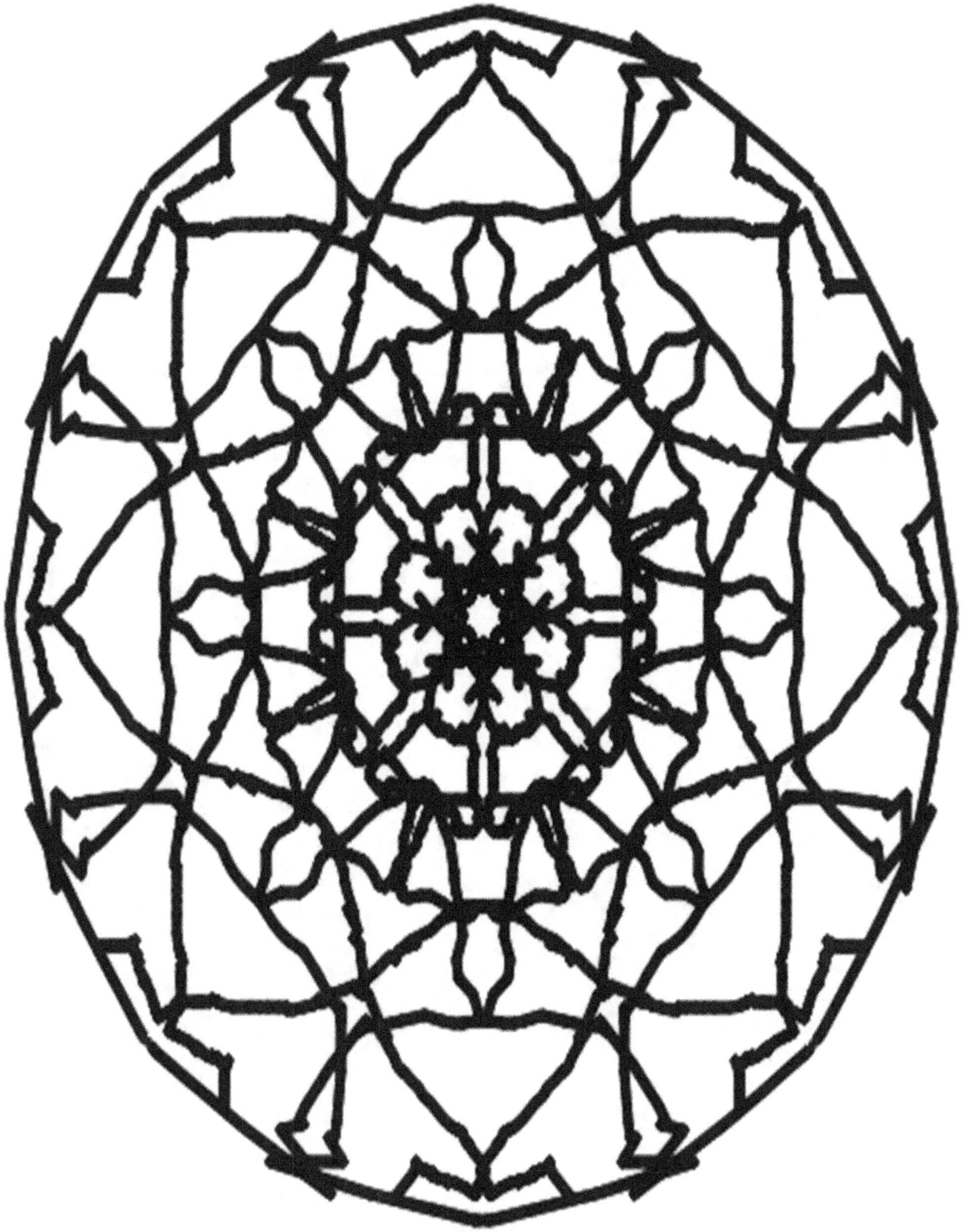

www.ingramcontent.com/pod-product-compliance
Lightning Source LLC
Chambersburg PA
CBHW081508170526
45166CB00008B/2592
* 9 7 8 1 5 1 9 2 7 2 3 1 7 *